INTENTIONAL CONNECTIONS

A Practical Guide to Parent Engagement in Early Childhood & Lower Elementary Classrooms

Dorothy Harman

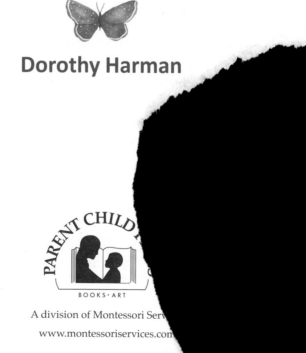

A division of Montessori Serv

www.montessoriservices.com

ISBN# 978-0-939195-60-2 (Paperback Edition)
ISBN# 978-0-939195-61-9 (eBook Edition)

Library of Congress Control Number 2018959175

Editor: Carey Jones
Photography: Brenda Peters
Butterfly Artwork: Carol Sapp
ercolor: Kjpargeter - Freepik.com

rinted in USA

t Printing 2018

BOOKS·ART

division of Montessori Services
www.montessoriservices.com

Lovingly dedicated to Mother and Daddy,
who taught me to value relationships and be of service to others.

Table of Contents

Foreword

Intentional Connections reflects Dorothy Harman's many years of teaching experience, as well as her personal philosophy about how to effectively engage parents in their child's life at school. When so often our encounters with parents are challenging, and may even include uneasy disagreements or conflicts, parent engagement can positively affect school communities and culture. This book offers activities that contribute to strong foundations on which teachers can build partnerships with parents, encouraging them to become active participants in their child's education. Dorothy also provides teachers with an understanding and appreciation of how engaged parents can strengthen our classrooms and make our work as educators more effective.

As Dorothy tells us, when we see parents as resources for our work with their children and attempt to develop the relationship, the benefits are real and lasting for us, for them, and most importantly, for their children.

Intentional Connections draws us in to discover new avenues and to find a renewed belief in ourselves as teachers and members of our communities. Beyond Dorothy's personal testimonies, she very adroitly provides the rationale for her techniques, anchoring her book securely in relevant research findings. And yet, this book is engaging! Her descriptions of interactions with parents provide us with clear illustrations of how relationships evolve and how those relationships ultimately benefit all.

For teachers just beginning their journey, this book will be invaluable. To those of us who also have years of teaching experience, Dorothy offers us an opportunity to renew our strengths and a chance to bring new ideas and excitement to our profession.

Intentional Connections will help teachers prepare for educating the children of the future.

Lavonne K. Plambeck, Ph.D.
Administrative Director, Mid-America Montessori Teacher Training Institute
Omaha, Nebraska

Introduction

I wish a book like *Intentional Connections* had been available to guide me through my first year of teaching. As a new teacher, I was terrified at the prospect of working with parents. I am not a naturally outgoing person. Speaking to a group of parents at a meeting or greeting new parents at an open house used to create anxious feelings in my stomach.

Perhaps a parent's school experience did not leave them with happy memories, so they arrive at their child's school feeling they need to defend their child, or perhaps they are struggling with parenting for a variety of reasons, wishing they had the support of an expert, but they are unsure how to ask for help. Dorothy's activities can be the first line of communication and connection between parents and teachers, and this connection and communication can make a world of difference to families in need of support.

Parent engagement fosters community, which is so needed in this world that often seems intent on creating division, isolation, and alienation.

I have known Dorothy for many years—as a Montessori early childhood teacher, trainer, colleague, and as a parent. My youngest daughter Bethany had the benefit of being in Dorothy's early childhood class. One of her favorite activities was hosting Bud the Bear.

I see *Intentional Connections* as absolutely invaluable. It expands the ability of a teacher to develop authentic community and bring people together. And, best of all, it shows us how to have fun while doing this important work.

Kathy Ziegler, M.A., M.Div.
Mid-America Montessori Teacher Training Institute
Omaha, Nebraska

In Praise of *Intentional Connections*

I grew up "Montessori" and during part of my childhood, Dorothy Harman was my teacher. Dorothy was always compassionate and caring, and the classroom was always a fun place to be. Fast forward twenty years to my Montessori Early Childhood training and Dorothy once again became my teacher. During my training, I learned many of Dorothy's strategies and activities—the same ones my family benefited from when I was a child.

It is challenging for children to reach their full potentials if school and home do not cooperate and work together. Throughout my time as a teacher, however, I have observed a gap that can exist between home and school. This gap is widened by a lack of parent engagement.

In our society today, parents can easily feel alienated, which can cause them to be highly critical of themselves, other parents, or teachers. This can lead to conflict. Creating opportunities to build community between families in the classroom is so important—it allows people to cultivate positive and supportive relationships, which in turn benefits all—including teachers!

Developing trust between teachers and parents helps bridge the gap between home and school. When a child is more fully supported, their academic success will increase, their confidence will rise, their behavior can improve, and often they will exhibit a more positive attitude toward school in general. Children can only benefit when parents and teachers work together.

Now as a Montessori teacher, I continue to benefit from Dorothy's model. I wish that all people could have her as their teacher. I know *Intentional Connections* will give people a taste of her vibrant spirit.

Bethany Ziegler
Infant/Toddler and Early Childhood Teacher, Montessori Education Centers
Omaha, Nebraska

He was shy; she was not.

He was quiet; she was not.

He was reserved; she was not.

He was bright, and so was she, and they deserved a school setting that honored and engaged them both.

You may conclude that this story was about two children. In actuality, the story is about a child and his mother who entered my early childhood classroom and became part of a teaching experience that shaped my career.

I was the teacher/director of a small private school where we developed a "village" in which to raise our children. We celebrated together, we had science fairs together, we took field trips together, and we built learning experiences together (including a gold mine and panning experience complete with spray-painted gold nuggets and cardboard box mine shafts!).

The activities were not as important as the "we" and "together" philosophy that was conceived in that setting. It has been my method of teaching ever since.

He became a sensitive young man who once wrote to thank me for instilling in him "a love of learning and reading."

She has been my best friend for more than 20 years.

Prologue

"My son is going to this amazing preschool. He's become so independent and is learning about countries all over the world. Don't you teach preschool, too? Have you ever heard of Montessori? Do you think you'd like to see my son's school?"

As a matter of fact, I was an early childhood major in college and worked in a private preschool. I had not heard much about Montessori—she and her method of education were mentioned in a college textbook. Sure, I needed to do an observation for one of my classes. So, what could it hurt?

At that time, I did not know that this observation would lead to a professional epiphany, my life's work, my story told on these pages, and a philosophy that I so dearly love that it would later shape the parenting of my own children and my personal life journey. The beauty I witnessed in that classroom resonated deeply within me. This was an environment intended to develop the whole child—the human "being," not just the human "doing." Maria Montessori wrote:

> Our care of the child should be governed, not by the desire "to make him learn things," but by the endeavor always to keep burning within him that light which is called intelligence. (Montessori, 1965, p. 240)

A few short years after that observation, I found myself the mother of two beautiful children in an area of California where the public school system struggled for resources. I chose to homeschool my kindergarten-age daughter, Alicia. My son, Anthony, was three, and I assumed he would benefit from the rich learning environment I was preparing for homeschooling. The news that a certified teacher was preparing a homeschool for preschool and kindergarten-age children traveled quickly through the small community. The inquiries of other parents resulted in a non-traditional homeschool that included a morning kindergarten class of six children and a preschool class of four in the afternoon.

With those ten children came their families. These were families who chose an intimate learning setting where field trips became extended family outings, collaboration built a western mining town out of cardboard boxes, partnership aided children in learning to ride bikes, and the community developed awe as we watched the birth of a litter of baby mice. I was entrusted with the privilege and responsibility of helping raise these amazing children. Although I was not yet Montessori trained, the desire to be more than a purveyor of concepts propelled me. I wanted to touch lives.

That same year, another Montessori classroom observation in Nebraska (of all unexpected places) reignited my commitment to become a Montessori teacher. At the end of my magical school year in 1997 in California, I moved to Omaha where I enrolled my children in a public Montessori school setting. Then I reshaped my career by completing Montessori training in 2001.

Yet, the families of those ten children in California remained with me spiritually. I wanted to create the same intimacy I experienced previously, because regardless of the setting, that same privilege and responsibility remained. Now, in my new professional setting, I had the opportunity to implement parental engagement with more diverse and numerous families.

I was fortunate to be hired as a teacher for a newly developed half-day classroom at the public school my children attended. The new classroom was filled with 18 children of parents who worked part-time or worked at home. The rapport with parents developed naturally. Many were able to volunteer in the classroom or visit during drop-off and pick-up times.

The following year I was hired to take on a full-day classroom with 44 children, most of whom had full-time working parents. I knew my approach would have to be dramatically different. So, I began to develop and search for new ways and methods to connect with parents. I sought graduate classes on building community and followed my natural inclinations to connect with others.

Eleven years into my Montessori career, I was flattered to be asked to begin training aspiring Montessorians. One of the early childhood courses I was asked to teach was a class about parent involvement. In a desire to deliver the course most effectively, I researched parent involvement. What I found affirmed not only the importance of working with families, but also the dramatic impact and long-term benefits parental engagement could make beyond the early childhood classroom.

It would be an untruth to state that every relationship with parents developed easily and that there weren't trials throughout the journey. I've had plenty of encounters, disappointments, learning opportunities, and even heartache. Make no mistake, teaching can be challenging. My experiences in public schools with curriculum requirements, tests and measures, and accountability have sometimes been overwhelming. Criticism can run high and teachers can feel isolated by the pressures. It seems teachers are often asked, "Can you attend one more meeting?" or "Can you add one more responsibility to your list of commitments?"

Building relationships with parents is not just "one more thing." It is a valuable investment in supporting one another and enriching the lives of children. Surprisingly, the first step in the process requires no work at all. It is simply a change of perspective about relationships with parents. It's kind of a "butterfly effect," where one small action can have a tremendous impact on a larger situation.

My most recent Montessori journey has included the good fortune of sharing my findings, methods, and passion for connecting with families at several national conferences. One of those opportunities resulted in the development of the book before you, through which I hope you become so familiar with my children that, as one editor once told me, "you can practically smell them." I hope you will join me on this ride and feel the rumble of deep intentional connections with others along your life's journey. I hope to inspire you, but mostly, I hope to celebrate your efforts (maybe with a little confetti) as you inspire and touch the lives of others.

May you have fun, learn lots, and make new friends through the ideas shared here.

Dorothy Harman
Omaha, Nebraska
September 2018

Chapter I
Why Parent Engagement Matters

Cindy's mom had a dusting of baking soda on her jeans; the smell of vinegar wafted through the classroom. When she mixed the two ingredients the group of three-to-six year-old children seated around her erupted in a collective "Whoa!" Their squeals of delight masked the sound of the gas bubbles as they exploded and oozed over the side of the vase. "Do it again! Can I try? That's cool!" Cindy grinned; she had done this experiment with her mom before. Cindy's mom beamed, because she had just shared her passion for chemistry with a group of eager young children who could hardly wait to try the experiment for themselves.

After reading this wonderful example of parent participation in my classroom, you might be surprised to learn that just a few weeks earlier, I was afraid to check my email for fear of finding yet another flurry of critical messages from this mother. She seemed driven to question my methods, my devotion to her child, and my understanding of her child's abilities. She and her husband were bright and well-educated. They valued academic success, and she used her title, *Dr.,* in all communications. Cindy's parents fiercely wanted what was best for their little girl; perhaps they thought that trying to micromanage me would get her the best possible education.

My first response was to reply politely to the emails, offering context, explanations, and even reassurances—to no effect. It seemed I had encountered "that parent" whom I'd never please. Cindy was new to my classroom, and I wondered if her parents' feelings were possibly affecting her own feelings about school.

I invited Cindy's mother to meet with me face to face. At our meeting, I presented all of my professional credentials and certifications, my personal philosophy of education, and an overview of my teaching experiences. I told her that I saw great promise in her daughter's work. I explained what I had in mind for Cindy and for the class in the coming months. I asked if she would be interested in sharing some of her skills and knowledge with our class. In short, I showed her that I valued the same things she valued—professional expertise, academic achievement, and, most importantly, her daughter's well-being.

At the end of our conversation, I asked her, "Can you trust me as an educator?"

Her answer was, "Yes."

The micromanaging emails stopped. For the rest of the school year, we collaborated on a number of wonderful, age-appropriate lessons related to both science and culture. This parent became a familiar face in my classroom. The whole class benefited from her participation, and her daughter thrived academically and socially.

In the short term, refusing to deal with this issue head-on might have helped me avoid some discomfort, but in the long run it would have been harmful to the child and her parents (and would have increased my sense of dread every time I checked my email).

The Benefits of Parent Engagement

As teachers, we know that building relationships with parents is important, but we aren't always certain how to develop rapport. Our own perceptions and the views of those around us can influence our attitudes toward parents. If you sometimes hear statements at your school that begin with "Those parents ..." or "They ought to ...", it's very likely the quality of the interactions may be challenging. Well-intentioned teachers often succumb to these sentiments for the simple reason that so much of our culture is steeped in polarity. We see it in political arenas and in gender and race relations. It may seem natural to see others as adversarial or oppositional. However, if we do the work to develop relationships with parents, it's easier to see them as resources and partners. And the benefits are real and lasting for teachers, parents, and, most importantly, children. One national organization tells us:

> The most accurate predictors of student achievement in school are not family income or social status, but the extent to which the family creates a home environment that encourages learning, communicates high yet reasonable expectations for the child's achievement and becomes involved in the child's education at school. (National PTA, 2000, pp. 11–12)

Others have concluded that parent engagement may be a stronger indicator of school success than parents' level of education (Henderson and Mapp, 2002), and the more intensely and intentionally parents are involved, the more beneficial and long-term the effects are.

While children spend a great deal of time in our educational settings, they still spend roughly seventy percent of their waking time outside of the school setting with families (Michigan Department of Education, 2001). As education professionals, we pride ourselves on our knowledge of child development and educational theory and practice, but we must not forget that parents are the foremost experts on their own children. As such, our work must complement the work parents do at home. Parents and teachers, working together with the child's best interests in mind, can have an invaluable and positive effect on the life of a child.

The long-term benefits of the parent-teacher relationship for the child include improved test scores, higher grades, more consistent attendance, increased self-esteem, and greater motivation in a school setting (Dervarics & O'Brien, 2011). The research also suggests that the earlier the parent-teacher-child relationship begins, the greater the benefit to the child (Weiss and Lopez, 2006). In addition, those parents who become engaged during their child's early years are more likely to remain involved. Thus, infant, toddler, early childhood, and lower elementary teachers have a great responsibility when it comes to engaging parents and creating positive experiences: this impact will persist for many more years.

Parent Engagement in Comparison to Parent Involvement

Involvement is usually defined as an act of doing "for" another. It is often a one-way encounter or dialogue. The youth who bags your groceries has involvement with you. Engagement, however, goes deeper; it is a mutually enhancing relationship, with all parties invested in the outcome. To enlist parents as partners is an example of engagement. Engagement supports the child's learning, confirms the teachers' efforts, and empowers parents through a relationship that demonstrates sincere care for their child's academic and social/emotional growth. Parents, teachers, and children benefit from open dialogue and mutual support, both when celebrating success and when facing challenges.

The Child-Parent-Teacher Relationship

Maria Montessori wrote extensively about the connection between the child, the teacher, and the prepared environment. The child's developmental readiness is the focus within a physical environment that helps develop independence, self-direction, and freedom. It contains a prepared teacher who can "visualize the child that is not yet there ... and [who] will reveal himself through work." (Montessori, 1946, p. 87). I believe the prepared environment extends beyond the physical environment to include the emotional environment of the child-parent-teacher relationship, an emotional environment that requires the same deliberate attention and intention as preparing a physical space.

When a teacher engages with a parent, it sends a message to children that their education is connected in a meaningful way to life outside of school. Common expectations delivered with common language by parents and teachers can demonstrate this home-school connection to the child. Beyond facilitating learning, teachers who have engaged with parents can be a seamless source of comfort, support, and guidance to the children in their care.

Sensitivity to the Hurdles of Parent Engagement

The benefits of an engaged relationship between parent, teacher, and child are numerous and well documented. Each individual gains through the commitment and coming together of the group. What the professional literature often lacks, however, are practical ideas for bridging the gap between home and school. Teachers may be resistant to add "one more thing" to their already demanding schedules. Likewise, parents are busy with the stresses and strains of raising children while in many cases working full-time to support their families.

In this book, I will bridge that gap by approaching common early childhood and lower elementary practices from a new perspective, offering strategies to create a mutually respectful engagement that feels like an investment, rather than a drag on time or resources. It is my intention for teachers and parents to consider a shift in perspective about the parent-teacher relationship.

Chapter II
Getting to Know Each Other:
Greeting Families with Purpose & Keeping
the Lines of Communication Open All Year

It's the Open House before the beginning of a new school year. Families arrive with their children — some are shy, some chatty, some nervous, and some excited. Every attempt has been made to make the classroom inviting. Shelves are pristine and arranged with deliberate care; each cubby and coat hook bears a child's name. Neat stacks of handouts sit on a child-size table and await the hands of parents. Building on the teacher's warm smile, kind greeting, and confident handshake, the teacher's handouts contain a wealth of information to share with parents: classroom expectations and procedures, school policies, lunch routines, and transportation methods, to name a few. Most importantly, a handout is the first line of written communication with new families.

Since face-to-face interactions may be limited to occasions of an open house or parent-teacher conference, effective written communication bears a great deal of the weight of building rapport with parents. Written communications require preparation and thought. A well-worded note can simply communicate information, but a poorly written piece can create opportunity for scrutiny of the teacher's professionalism. Well-chosen language speaks volumes!

Sharing Your Intentions (Mission Statement)

"Have fun. Learn lots. Make new friends." It's the phrase my children, Alicia and Anthony, heard from me throughout most of their educational career, including their years of university studies. At first, it seemed like one of those plucky mom-isms, delivered with a hug before the beginning of a new day, semester, or school year, but I came to realize it was also my own educational and personal epigram or mission statement. It's brief and clear, communicates my beliefs, values, and goals surrounding education, and reminds me of my role and responsibility to fulfill that mission.

"Have fun." I believe learning should be a joyful journey, not a final destination.

"Learn lots." I believe learning is a lifelong process that occurs both within and beyond the classroom.

"Make new friends." I believe relationships matter, especially because we have so much to learn from one another.

I encourage all teachers to come up with their own personal mission statement. Yours need not be as lofty as Walt Disney's original and famous mission: "Make people happy." Still, a mission statement will help to communicate your expectations and values to parents. Thankfully, it's not nearly as lengthy as the personal philosophy of education paper that many of us had to write at some point in our teacher training, though that paper may help.

I like to utilize two or three ideas that are easily remembered and are simple and clear to communicate. You may note that I used brevity and simple language that children can understand and repeat, so it can be included as part of a greeting at the beginning of the day. You may also wish to communicate your mission in a letter of introduction, an email, a newsletter, or a webpage.

Welcoming Your Community of Learners for the First Time

You only get one first impression. Many teachers are naturally gregarious, and for them relationships and conversation come easily. Others are more introverted, and the idea of facing parents at an open house or other back-to-school event makes them a bit uncomfortable. Regardless of your personality type, the first contact with a child's family is important.

Forbes magazine suggests five strategies for making a positive first impression. Those include setting a clear intention prior to the event, attending to your appearance, being mindful of body language, being aware of your own mood, and perhaps most importantly for a teacher, being interested in the child and family (Van Petten, 2011).

I like to greet parents with eye contact and a quick hello as I am kneeling to greet their child at eye level. I believe it is important to ask the child's permission to shake their hand, and then I introduce myself. Initiating conversation with the child is my first priority and is usually based upon something observable such as the design on a t-shirt or backpack. I greet parents more formally and share the packet of handouts with them once the conversation with the child has concluded.

One of my handouts is a letter to families. It begins with a sincere welcome that states my intentions. I pay particular attention to word choice. The first line reads: "We are very excited about your family joining our family at Montclair Elementary School."

The use of the word "family" to describe our school offers a glimpse into my philosophy. Other handouts include a letter of introduction, a class schedule, ways to support students at home, arrival/dismissal procedures, parent-teacher conference dates, a schedule of when and how to anticipate newsletters, and my email address.

Organization, grammar, spelling, and brevity are important considerations when compiling materials for this first meeting with families. Booklets with a wealth of information are overwhelming and are frequently overlooked by busy families. (I think of the volumes of information in my own children's high school handbooks that I honestly never read.) Brief weekly email newsletters kept me abreast of the flurry of activities in their schools.

I try to keep the open house handouts to three or four pages. Brief and frequent communications throughout the year are more likely to be read and keep parents wanting more.

Letters of Introduction

There are few things as intimidating or embarrassing as being asked to write about oneself. "How do I begin?" you might wonder. "What do I say?" "I'm really not comfortable talking about myself." These may be some of the many excuses for not writing a letter of introduction to share with your families. But, as in many of my strategies for developing communication, once it's written, it only needs to be saved, and can easily be updated as needed.

For a letter of introduction, I follow just a few rules:

- Note my years at the school. It's an easy way to begin.
- List some of my accomplishments.
- Include a bit of my personal life.
- Keep it brief—a page or less!

Why include details about your personal life? Because it makes you relatable and will help initiate positive interactions! If you are having trouble coming up with what to include about yourself, take a look at the list of topics below, and then choose a few that are applicable to your life. In my experience, I often find connection with parents when I list my hobbies and the places I've taught. Whatever information you choose to include, remember that the idea is to develop the relationship between yourself and your families. Your openness begins that connection. So don't be shy!

- Name
- Significant other's name
- Children's or grandchildren's name(s)
- Where are you from?
- Do you have brothers and sisters?
- Do you have any pets? What kind? Names?
- Number of years working with children at this school or other schools

- Favorite part of your job
- Hobbies
- Birthday (year not necessary)
- Favorite color
- Favorite food, beverage, or restaurant

This is the letter of introduction I shared with parents in 2016:

Dear Parents,

Welcome to Montclair Elementary School and to my classroom. I am blessed to be joined by two assistants, Mrs. Walters and Mrs. Volvoicar. Combined, we have more than 26 years of experience in teaching Montessori at this school.

This begins my 20th year at Montclair where I have been both a parent and a teacher. My children attended the school through eighth grade. My daughter, Alicia, is a graduate of the University of Kansas and is attending graduate school in Melbourne, Australia. My son, Anthony, is a recent graduate of the University of Nebraska-Lincoln. He is employed by the Nebraska Humane Society. I have two stepdaughters, Katina and Lara, and a granddaughter, Adelya, who live in Germany. My second grandchild is due in March. My husband, Chris, attends many school functions, as he is often recruited to help with our All-School Play, Poetry Slam, Paints and Pastries, and school carnival!

I first discovered the Montessori philosophy in a college textbook as I was completing my bachelor's degree. My teaching and life experiences have taken me many places. I've lived and taught in Michigan, Mississippi, Virginia, California, and Germany. I've completed two master's degrees, in education and creative arts, and I've taught in private schools and Department of Defense schools. When my children were young, I also ran a small school out of my home, teaching ten students.

Omaha became home for my children and me when I moved here to pursue Montessori training and have my children attend public school Montessori at Montclair. Now I spend my summers training new Montessori teachers. I've found I enjoy teaching adults almost as much as I love guiding children in my Montessori classroom. This school year, I will be a presenter at a Montessori conference in Florida. I'm also working on a book for teachers, through Parent Child Press, that will stress the importance of parent engagement. So, watch for many opportunities to become involved in our classroom in and out of school this year!

My other interests include writing and directing children's theater, reading, sewing, walking, gardening, attending hockey games, serving as an associate pastor at my church, playing percussion and singing in two tribute bands, watching movies (especially Pixar films — Toy Story and Monsters, Inc. are my favorites!), going to the New Jersey Shore (the place,not the reality show!), where I visit my older brother and sister. My passions include environmental conservation, peace education, ministry, motorcycles, and Montessori!

My favorite color is orange and my favorite food is a Starbucks mocha, which is technically not a food, but you'll still see me with my reusable coffee cup full of chocolate coffee most Wednesdays!

It is my great privilege to work and learn with your children. I hope to provide them with experiences that expand their knowledge and skills, develop their love of learning, and promote joy.

In love and service,
Mrs. Harman

Newsletters

For some teachers, writing a classroom newsletter throughout the year seems like a labor-intensive project with few returns. They believe parents won't read them, so teachers conclude newsletters aren't worth the effort. I've found, however, that newsletters are a great help in engaging parents. They provide information for parents about events in the classroom and describe activities deliberately planned for parent engagement (discussed in Chapter IV, *Extending Classroom Experiences*, p. 36). My newsletters also provide parent-child talking points about the school day.

I write a weekly newsletter, using a digital template, which makes the process go faster for me. I include classroom pictures, which parents always love to see. Finally, I deliver my newsletter at the same time and in the same way each week, making it easy for parents to anticipate.

Like most teachers, I don't have a great deal of spare time. I'm able to make a weekly newsletter work because I have a strategy of "upcycling." I save my weekly newsletters from year to year and usually find that each document only requires a few brief updates, like date changes for events and edits for children's names. The school year flows in a predictable rhythm that lends itself to upcycling. For example, the classroom Halloween party happens each October, but the dates and times may change. School fundraisers fall at approximately the same time each year, but the dates may change. By upcycling, the updates are quick, usually taking less than 15 minutes to complete. See sample newsletter on page 14.

Another method for newsletter writing is "scrolling." New information is inserted as the first item in a list and old information scrolls downward until it no longer appears in the document. For example, the newsletter may have the following headings:

Field Trip Planned for November 18
Thank you for attending Parent-Teacher Conferences.
Fall has arrived! Be sure to wear a jacket to school.

The subsequent newsletter may read:

Donations Being Accepted for our Canned Food Drive (new item)
Field Trip Planned for November 18
Thank you for attending Parent-Teacher Conferences.

("Fall has arrived! Be sure to wear a jacket to school." is now deleted from the document.)

Newsletters are only effective if they are read, so I have developed several strategies that help ensure this is the case. I make each newsletter available in three ways—an email, a hard copy, and an archived digital version, so parents can choose the medium that best fits their needs. Next, I deliver the document at the same time each week. Parents know that a newsletter will be in their email inbox each Friday afternoon, and the subject line will always read "Mrs. Harman's Newsletter" (this makes it easy to recognize in the inbox, and also makes it simple to search for later). I also include a hard copy of the newsletter in each child's "Friday Folder" (which goes home on Friday afternoon). Finally, all of my past newsletters are archived online.

As mentioned above, I've found that including photographs in the newsletter increases readership. Parents and children alike are aware that each week I include photographs of students working in the classroom or playing on the playground. Children always love to look at the newsletter to see if they are there, and this motivates parents to take a peek as well.

We live in an age where communications are essential and rapid. Technology and the use of parent information apps can allow parents to feel involved and informed about their children's activities throughout the day. Many teachers use online communication sites that allow photos, videos, and texts to be delivered instantly to parents' devices.

Photographs speak volumes when used to communicate with parents. Keep in mind, however, that you must have a parent's permission before photographing children. Address this issue early on by including a permission form with classroom registration paperwork. Your school may already have a blanket photo permission form. If not, here's the one I use:

<u>Picture Permission</u>

Occasionally, children may be photographed in our classroom for the purposes of parent communication and classroom projects.

Please check and sign below if your child's picture may be used for these purposes.

Or check and sign the denial box if you wish to have your child's picture excluded from these projects.

Return form to school.

☐ Mrs. Harman may use my child's picture in parent communication and classroom projects.

_____ child's name

_____ parent's signature

☐ Please do not use my child's picture.

_____ child's name

_____ parent's signature

Here's a sample newsletter using my digital template:

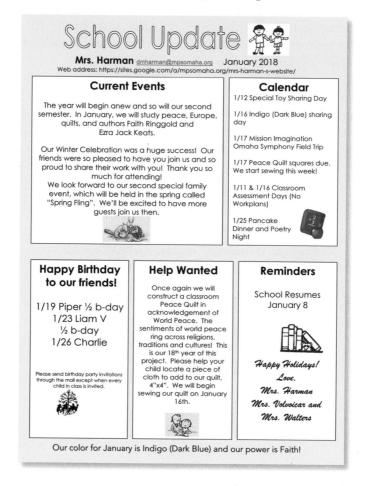

Parent Education Opportunities

Parents have innumerous professional, personal, and vocational skills, but it is rare that they can match our expertise as teachers in the subjects of early childhood development and education. I've often witnessed teachers who are frustrated about parents' lack of early childhood knowledge. Those same teachers, however, don't get frustrated by children's lack of knowledge or experience. Instead of faulting parents for their deficits, we can seize them as opportunities for instruction.

While parents are the authorities on their children's unique needs, teachers can help provide a framework of norms for parents to work from. Parent education is especially important in non-traditional educational settings such as Montessori; few parents have personal experience to refer back to.

I like to initiate partnership with parents by asking them why they chose Montessori. Through discussion, we ascertain the underlying values behind their decision. I congratulate them for taking action on their children's education; it's a clear indication that they are committed to providing the best for their child. I use it as an opportunity to relate this commitment to the choices they make within their family and at home. I discuss my expectation that we will all work and learn together for mutual benefit. This conversation illuminates a path that leads to many opportunities for further parent education.

There are many methods of providing parent education, including on-site school events, articles from professional or educational publications, and virtual meetings. I find that meetings that have a social component (and include childcare), such as potlucks or family fun nights, result in the greatest attendance.

Brief, concise, and well-organized presentations with opportunities for questions and answers are most effective and encourage repeat attendance. I like to present broad topics at the beginning of the school year, when such meetings are most attended, and specific topics throughout the rest of the year.

I also keep a running archive of articles to share throughout the year, and I'm always adding new pieces to it. Publications such as *Tomorrow's Child*, *Montessori Life*, and Montessori Services' *Ideas and Insights* provide a wealth of information for my Montessori parents. These publications can benefit children in any learning environment.

"Bright Spot" Emails

As a means of reaffirming the teacher-parent relationship, I send a monthly "Bright Spot" email: a brief message of encouragement. A Bright Spot could include an image or quote, an uplifting meme from social media, or a photo of a child working in my classroom accompanied by a quote or reflection. I gather quotes over the summer break or as time allows during the school year. And just as I do with my newsletters, I save my old Bright Spot messages and reuse effective ones with only slight changes.

Cosmos is a Greek Word for the Order of the Universe. It is in a way, the opposite of Chaos. It implies the deep interconnectedness of all things. It conveys awe for the intricate and subtle way in which the universe is put together.

~Carl Sagan

An example of a Bright Spot Email using an image from the classroom and a quote from Cosmos *(Sagan, 2013, p. 17).*

Observation Checklists

Observation is a cornerstone of the scientific method and helps us to not only objectively identify behavior, but also identify the needs of a child so we can better meet the needs moving forward. Taking the time to objectively observe student behavior can be enlightening for a teacher, and these observations can also serve as a useful tool during communication with parents. While most of these observations are routine, occasionally they confirm a concerning pattern of behavior.

Every day I try to observe two to three children. I observe at the same time each day, when children are working independently. I carry a clipboard that is peppered with stickers on the back as my indicator to the children that I am observing them work and am not to be interrupted. As with any procedure, the children become accustomed to this. These observations require only a couple of minutes to complete, yet are a valuable snapshot of each child at work in the classroom. These snapshots can provide evidence of patterns over a period of time and can become a focal point of discussion with parents.

When undesirable patterns need to be discussed with a parent, this documentation can be a valuable tool for communicating about specific observed behaviors. This is often more effective than generalized statements, such as "she's always untidy with materials." A procedure for observations could include preparing a stack of observation sheets with children's names already labeled on them. Keep the sheets in random order. The child whose sheet is on the top is the child to observe next.

Life Skills Observation

Child's Name _____ Date: _____

Time: _____

Practicing these skills		Needs More Practice
_____	1. manages time	_____
_____	2. follows directions	_____
_____	3. solves problems	_____
_____	4. cooperates with others	_____
_____	5. concentrates on work	_____
_____	6. chooses work independently	_____
_____	7. demonstrates responsibility	_____
_____	8. sets goals	_____
_____	9. seeks help	_____
_____	10. demonstrates care for others	_____
_____	11. takes ownership of actions	_____
_____	12. accepts consequences	_____
_____	13. positive attitude	_____
_____	14. self-control of emotions	_____
_____	15. self-control of body	_____
_____	16. keeps trying	_____
_____	17. orderly in care of materials	_____
_____	18. speaks kindly	_____
_____	19. respects others' work	_____
_____	20. listens to others	_____

Additional Comments:

Observation checklist developed with Millard Public Schools

Anecdotal Observations

Anecdotal observations can be a part of the daily observation record (as part of the "Additional Comments" section), or they can be made separately on a blank piece of paper. Anecdotal observations require more time to complete, though with practice, they go faster. They are particularly helpful when communicating specific concerns to a parent.

For example, Jackie was a girl who was trying out some disparaging language with other children in my classroom. I first attempted to engage her parents with my concern; our discussions, however, seemed to be inadequate to resolve the problem. I wrote her name on my observation sheet, hoping to gather information that would help me communicate more effectively with her parents. I closely recorded each word she said while I appeared to be watching another child working. I created the ruse since I hoped her language or behavior would not be altered by my presence. (To save valuable writing time and to protect the privacy of the other children in case a student happens to come by and glance at what I'm writing, I list names as initials.) Below is an example of my observation of Jackie.

Anecdotal observation sample:

> J: placing pegs into pegboard while working at a table
> J: returns pegs to basket
> J: returns work to the shelf
> S: coloring at another table
> J: walks over and says, "I don't like your picture."
> S: (continues to color)
> J: "Red is ugly."
> S: "I like red."
> J: "Throw it away!"
> S: "Leave me alone or I'm telling."
> J: shrugs shoulders, rolls eyes, and walks away

This objective observation opened the door for a new conversation with Jackie's parents. They agreed that this type of language was not helping Jackie make friends and was hurtful to other children. We worked together to develop a plan. Jackie's parents committed to limiting Jackie's exposure to TV programming that glamorized adolescent female bullying. We aligned our efforts and language to support Jackie's appropriate social communication.

Note that anecdotal observations should be as objective as possible. Report only those behaviors that can be seen and heard; never try to guess the motivations or feelings behind children's behaviors.

At the same time, record observations that demonstrate appropriate or on-task behaviors. They provide reflections of moments in the child's day that a parent would be delighted to recognize.

Daily, Weekly, or Monthly Reports

Another way to communicate information about a child's day and work habits is via a written work plan that can be completed by the teacher or the child. The samples below allow writing space for planned lessons, completed lessons, and "random acts of kindness" to document the child's day or week.

Monthly work plans allow for work habits to be demonstrated. For example, you may note that José has completed his math work each day for the month, but hasn't completed any geography work. This information could help guide instruction and provide information that parents could use to encourage further exploration of a topic.

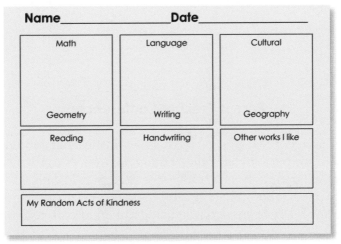

Daily Work Plan

Name_____**Date**_____

Week of:	Monday	Tuesday	Wednesday	Thursday	Friday
Math					
Geometry					
Language					
Writing					
Cultural					
Geography					
Reading					
Handwriting					

Week of:	Monday	Tuesday	Wednesday	Thursday	Friday
Math					
Geometry					
Language					
Writing					
Cultural					
Geography					
Reading					
Handwriting					

Week of:	Monday	Tuesday	Wednesday	Thursday	Friday
Math					
Geometry					
Language					
Writing					
Cultural					
Geography					
Reading					
Handwriting					

Week of:	Monday	Tuesday	Wednesday	Thursday	Friday
Math					
Geometry					
Language					
Writing					
Cultural					
Geography					
Reading					
Handwriting					

Weekly/Monthly Work Plan

Parent-Teacher Conferences

Few things unnerve teachers as much as parent-teacher conferences. They take hours to prepare for, and the actual conferences can consume whole school days, even though each conference itself may be only 15–30 minutes long. Parent expectations are high, and there is much to be shared in a short period of time. If I've been regularly using my other parent communication strategies, I find I have already shared a great deal of information, and I feel less pressure to rush through the conference.

I begin each conference with a handshake and a friendly greeting as though I'm meeting a friend, because I am! To get started, I ask parents to share. This breaks the ice and makes parents feel welcome. Some questions may include:

- "What does Max tell you about his school day?"
- "What is Saira's favorite part of school?
- "What friends are you hearing about the most?"
- "Did Jodie tell you about her accomplishment yesterday?"

Next, I share an observation about the child. I believe character traits and non-academic-based observations communicate a connection with the wholeness of the child. In addition, they are easy for parents to understand.

- "Yesterday, Rasheed said the funniest thing ..."
- "The other day, Martha showed such caring for her friends when ..."
- "Amaya was so ambitious when ..."
- "Joe was so patient when ..."
- "Henry was so excited to share ..."

Once the dialogue is open, I begin a deeper exchange of information. The Harvard Family Research Project (2010) suggests the "BE HEARD" strategy for conducting conferences.

*B*est intentions assumed
*E*mphasis on learning

*H*ome-school collaboration
*E*xamples and evidence
*A*ctive listening
*R*espect for all
*D*edication to follow-up

Many teachers like to prepare documentation prior to the conference. Assessment data, samples of work, and anecdotal records are valuable resources to share. Using a document like the one below can provide brief, concrete information about a child's strengths as well as opportunities for growth:

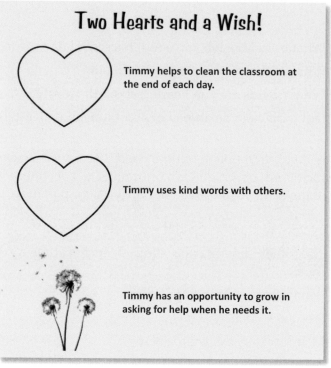

"Two Hearts and a Wish" for sharing at parent-teacher conferences

The "wish" part is perhaps the most critical item to share (and may be the most challenging one to bring up), but it should not consume the entire conference. Focus on the positive; this will create an atmosphere of collaboration and problem solving. Use statements that reinforce your partnership:

- "I believe we can work together on this opportunity."
- "I trust our combined efforts will serve Susie well."
- "I'm open to your suggestions."

Semantics matter in relationship building—word choice can greatly help you or greatly hurt you. Language that is accusatory, places blame, or shames parents will be met with opposition. Think of the conference as another chance to further develop the parent-teacher relationship and engage parents for the long-term benefit of the child.

Whether the "wishes" seem to outnumber the "hearts," it is important to always end a conference on a positive note. (See Chapter IX, *Addressing Challenges Together*, p. 117 for how to manage a more complicated or ongoing student issue or problem.) Affirming closing statements reinforce the relationship. Those could include:

- "I'm so looking forward to our year together."
- "Thank you for partnering with me."
- "It's been so helpful to spend this time together."

Staying in Contact

Open and honest communication is the foundation of a healthy relationship. Much of this chapter has focused on providing information to families (expressive communication), which is only part of the equation. Being open to receiving information from parents (receptive communication) is also essential.

I suggest developing clear guidelines for parent contact. Some teachers prefer handwritten notes, others phone calls, and still others prefer email. No matter the medium, let parents know how soon they can expect to hear back from you. For example, I prefer email as a means of communication, and I ask parents to provide me with 24 hours to respond to their inquiry. In some cases, this time window may not be enough, but I'll always respond within a day, saying something like, "Thank you for contacting me. I will need more time to adequately answer your question, but I will get back to you as soon as I possibly can."

A consistent "24-hour response rule" helps keep the flow of communication going and assures parents that their input is important and that you value the relationship.

Chapter III
Personal Touches:
Integrating Home into the Learning Environment

Samantha bounds into the classroom with joy and pride, clutching to her chest a treasured piece of pink fluffy fabric, cut from her outgrown pajamas.

William is distracted by another child's multi-colored zipper bag. He accidentally walks into a child-size chair. Not to worry, he was uninjured, and he didn't drop his painted, glitter-glued seashell!

It's been a difficult morning, and parting from her dad at the door brought sadness to Kara's somber four-year-old expression. Luckily, she has a photograph of him that she can hold throughout the day until the sadness fades. She may need it again during naptime, when she can place the photograph beside her on the nap mat.

My heart still warms when I think of all the hot summer nights I spent as a child on the front porch of our Victorian house. Remembering the sounds of the rocking chairs on the old porch floorboards and the jangle of the ice cubes in iced tea glasses still fills me with longing so many years later. This longing for home also resides within the children in our classrooms. Although, our classrooms are prepared with stimulating activities, a wealth of opportunities, and warm affection, home still beckons. Opportunities to bring a touch of home and family into the classroom soften that call.

"A good snapshot keeps a moment from running away." I love this quote by American writer Eudora Welty. If you check your phones, hard drives, photo albums, and scrapbooks, you'll be flooded with moments you cherish so dearly that you would never allow them to "run away." We call this experience nostalgia.

Nostalgia comes from a Greek word meaning "return home," and it is a physiological response in the brain that helps us connect with past experiences, remember places and events, and think about our relationships with others. For children in particular, thinking about their homes and families can ease difficult transitions. My intention with the activities described in this section is to create a connection between home and school and to integrate items from home into the learning environment. I begin with the most concrete representation of family: a photo. Then I provide objects for families to use to create Mini Masterpieces. Finally, families select and contribute something from home—fabric for the Peace Quilt and objects for the class Stepping Stone.

Family Photos

Framed family photos connect children to their homes, families, and memories, and also create a home-like feel in the classroom. Place the photos on shelves, counters, windowsills, or tables. They can be grouped with others or stand alone, as space and aesthetics allow. Maria Montessori named her first school Casa dei Bambini, or Children's House; the family photos in my classroom help to create a home-like atmosphere.

The photos elicit conversations about family members, family pets, and types of families. They extend relationships beyond the boundaries of the classroom. It's common to hear, "Hi, Bobby's dad" or "Hello, Alicia's abuela" at dismissal or at school functions. The photos help children begin to develop an understanding of extended family, and the deep connections we have with others.

I include photos of my own family in the classroom as well. My husband's photo and a photo of my 24-pound orange cat, Pumpkin, are particular favorites. The children often giggle as they wonder at the enormity of my cat! We also look at the photographs during group show-and-tell experiences. I ask one child at a time to tell us about their photograph. Then the other children can ask questions about the individuals and places pictured.

I take a very casual approach to managing the photographs. Some pictures will remain in the classroom the entire year, while others will be traded out for new snapshots. Though most images are photographs, we've had hand-drawn family portraits as well. Of course, some families choose not to participate. All responses are welcome; this is just one of many activities designed to engage families.

This is a sample family note that I include in one of my weekly newsletters at the beginning of the school year as children are adjusting to their classroom.

Our Class is a Home. During our group snack time we sing a special song that includes the lyrics, "I have my friends with me, like one big family!"

In that spirit, I'd like to create a home-like atmosphere in our classroom by adding a family touch. On our shelves, we will gladly display photographs of each child and their family.

The images may be snapshots, school pictures, collages, or even hand-drawn family portraits. The frames should be easel-backed or free standing. Please limit frame size to no larger than 5"x 7" so we can easily manage the display. Both photo and frame will be returned at the end of the year.

Please let us know if locating a frame or a photo is difficult as we have a few frames that have been donated to our classroom, and we'd be happy to take a family photo at one of our many school events.

Mini Masterpieces

When I began teaching at my current school twenty years ago, I inherited a room with one wall. Literally, one wall! My building was built during the 1970s, during the "open school" model of school construction. A few bookcases and a little imagination defined the end of one classroom and the beginning of the next.

This wasn't a tremendous problem, since I tended to keep my walls "quiet." I subscribe to the idea that too much clutter on the walls distracts children's attention from their work and the materials on the shelves. However, I did want my classroom to have aesthetic appeal, so I came up with a solution that I call Mini Masterpieces—small pieces of child-decorated items, arranged in a shadow box. They allow for a touch of beauty in an unobtrusive display.

A shadow box can be any type of display box with compartments. Mine is an antique printer's drawer with approximately sixty 1"x 1" compartments (it was around $20 on eBay; Etsy is another good source). Throughout the year, I collect a variety of small items. Children choose an item, I put their names on the back, and then they take it home to decorate, usually with the help of a family member. Once finished, each child brings the item back to school, and we place it in the shadow box for display.

Mini Masterpieces

As with the family photographs, children are invited to show the items and answer questions from the rest of the class about the masterpiece (usually a combination of questions that others have modeled, such as "Who helped you make it?" "How did you make it?" or "Why do you like it?"). Then children display the items in a compartment of their choosing. Some items remain all year, while others come and go, in a constantly changing display of children's and parents' artwork.

Young children are sensitive to detail and love little boxes. Some items I have found to fit in my shadow box compartments include:

- seashells
- rocks
- bottle caps
- small wooden items from a craft store—stars, hearts, cubes, wooden doll forms

Each item goes home in a small bag along with a note describing the activity. Typically, once the first painted seashell or bottle cap appears, the others will soon follow!

This is a sample family note I include in one of my weekly newsletters, along with the small object to be turned into a Mini Masterpiece:

I have a little HEART
It is so very plain.
Please decorate this heart,
And send it back again.

Please decorate the enclosed heart with any material you choose: paint, glue, glitter, stickers, markers, sequins, puff balls, poetry, pictures, etc.

The possibilities are unlimited, though your space is not.

Please return the decorated heart to Mrs. Harman by February 9 so your heart can be on display for our Valentine's party on February 14.

Peace Quilt

One of my favorite Practical Life activities to share with children is sewing. The skills of practical living such as pouring water, using tongs, bead stringing or sewing (to name a few) are excellent for developing fine motor skills, concentration, coordination, and independence. In my classroom, we practice running stitches, button sewing, bookbinding, making yarn dolls, and weaving.

Practical Life sewing experiences culminate in an opportunity to practice the nomenclature for the parts of a sewing machine. Our final project is an adult-guided experience with machine sewing: our Peace Quilt.

I ask each child to bring a swath of fabric to be added to the quilt. Most children bring in small pieces of old clothing or blankets, but others go on a special trip with their parents to a fabric store, where the child chooses a meaningful piece of fabric. Bringing in fabric is always a voluntary activity. I trust that parents will participate in these activities if they are able. I also keep additional pieces of fabric on hand in the classroom if children wish to choose from those.

Once all children have their fabric, we set a date for the quilt construction. This timing is also dependent upon my willingness to let go of general classroom responsibilities and machine-sew with the children. Having a parent volunteer helps. I'm lucky enough to have a parent who still volunteers in my classroom even though her daughter hasn't been there for five years. Building relationships works!.

On the quilt construction day, we all sit in a large circle and each child shares something they like about their fabric. When everyone has had a turn, we dim the lights, light a candle at the center of our circle, and recite the following dedication.

The children follow the teacher's lead, repeating the action and each line spoken:

Peace Quilt Dedication

(*hold fabric for all to see*)
This square is for the Peace Quilt
That hangs upon the wall.
It reminds me of love and kindness
Towards one and all.

(*place fabric on hands*)
The Peace Quilt reminds me to do kind deeds.

(*place fabric on ear*)
The Peace Quilt reminds me to listen for kind words.

(*place fabric by eyes*)
The Peace Quilt reminds me to watch for kind actions.

(*place fabric by mouth*)
The Peace Quilt reminds me to say kind words.

(*place fabric on top of head*)
The Peace Quilt reminds me to think kind thoughts.

(*place fabric on heart*)
The Peace Quilt reminds me to have a kind heart!

I then invite the children to "piece" the quilt by placing similar colors next to one another on the floor. I might say, "If your fabric has blue on it, please place them in a row with the other blue fabrics. If you have fabric with pink …"

The resulting effect is child-designed and always lovely. Finally, each child is welcomed, one at a time, to operate the sewing machine pedal and watch as an adult safely guides the fabric swaths through the sewing machine. The Peace Quilt is a charming and concrete demonstration of adults and children coming together to create a beautiful work of art!

We are currently constructing a second Peace Quilt. We began construction in 2011, and it will be completed in 2020. The first quilt took 10 years to construct and remains at my home; it is one of my most beloved teaching artifacts. I can even connect some of the fabric squares to specific children, and other squares are beautiful reminders of all the children who have moved through my classroom. One precious square belonged to a child whose funeral I attended after he tragically passed away in fifth grade.

The beauty of the quilt is not in the color or texture of the fabrics, but in the energies of families who shop for the perfect fabric or sacrifice a treasured piece of a child's blanket or outgrown clothing for this project. My dear friend (and publisher) Joe Campbell wrote of this project, "To be a part of something bigger than ourselves is what makes life meaningful. We all can give something valuable to integrate into a bigger, stronger and more beautiful tapestry."

Peace Quilt — Created by children and parents from 2000-2010

This is the note I send home to families each year before we begin the Peace Quilt project. I send it home prior to the first day of winter with the intention to have the fabric squares returned and sewn together during the week following the observation of the birthday of Dr. Martin Luther King, Jr. — a perfect time to focus on peace and peacemakers. The concept of a Peace Quilt is two-fold: it has the practical purpose of providing warmth in the winter and is symbolic of peace as the fabrics are brought together to form a unity.

Cloth of Many Colors Global Peace Project

On January 1, 2000, hundreds of volunteers gathered at the United Nations Building in New York City and encircled the outside of the building with a quilt constructed of pieces of fabric gathered from all over the world — including five hundred pieces contributed from our school.

From that experience, the Preprimary Peace Quilts were conceived. In 2000, we asked our students to donate two pieces of fabric. One piece of fabric was sent to the UN and the other was used to begin our classroom quilts.

Each beautifully unique quilt square is symbolic of a unique child in our program. We honor that uniqueness and marvel at the beauty of our quilt squares joined with quilt squares from other unique human beings from around the world. This is the symbolism of the Peace Quilt. We are individually beautiful, yet when we join with others, we create a work of art.

Each year since 2000, the children have donated squares to add to our quilts. Please help us continue this tradition by sending a 4" x 4" square of fabric to school with your child. The fabric means the most to those children who have helped to choose the cloth. It may be from an outgrown piece of clothing, an old sheet or blanket, or any other source of fabric. Please pencil your child's name on the back of the fabric; it is great fun for the children to identify their squares from years past.

As always, thank you so much for your help with this project and may your New Year be filled with peace!

Maria Montessori wrote of peace and unity:

> Times have changed, and science has made great progress, and so has our work; but our principles have only been confirmed, and along with them our conviction that mankind can hope for a solution to its problems, among which the most urgent are those of peace and unity, only by turning its attention and energies to the discovery of the child and to the development of the great potentialities of the human personality in the course of its formation. (Montessori, 1948, pp. ix-x.)

Stepping Stones

Another collective group project is crafting a Stepping Stone. Usually done in the spring, this activity creates another opportunity for children and parents to bring a touch of home into the classroom. The result is a delightful, family-inspired addition to the outdoor classroom environment or garden.

Simple stepping stone kits can be purchased from craft or hardware stores. I invite families and children to bring in a special stone, seashell, marble, mosaic or tile piece, or other non-perishable item that can be pressed into wet concrete as it begins to dry in a mold. Just as with the Peace Quilt project, I keep a supply of extra items on hand from which children may choose if they don't bring something from home. And just as with the Peace Quilt, I don't dwell on or keep track of which children bring in stones from home and which ones choose from my supply.

We construct our Stepping Stone each May as the irises are blooming outside the classroom windows and the school year is winding to a close. It becomes the final parent engagement activity. The marbles, rocks, seashells, and mosaic tiles make impressions in the concrete, just as we made impressions on each other while working together all year.

The children watch with delight as I mix the concrete powder with water to create the "mud" into which they press the treasures they chose with their parents. They observe the mud ooze around their objects. Then we use a stick to write the date and year in the wet cement to memorialize the children and families who have contributed to make each year's stepping stone. The children check on the mixture over the final days of school as the mud turns to stone and our days of being together for the year draw to a close.

I send this note home to families before we start our Stepping Stone project.

> Stepping Stone Construction!
>
> We'll be creating a Stepping Stone for our garden. Your child may bring a piece of mosaic tile, stone, or a marble to add to our Stepping Stone (please label with name in a sack).
>
> Our Stepping Stones are on display outside our classroom window!

One of our garden Stepping Stones

What Are the Benefits of Integrating Home into the Learning Environment?

By allowing children to bring pieces of their outside-of-school life into school, we are strengthening the partnership with families and creating a link between home and school. Tangible objects brought from home can serve as physical reminders of the people and things children love. Sharing stories about the people and places in their lives can help children build connections with others in their classroom. The cooperative projects presented here are just a few that can be implemented to engage parents and integrate home into the learning environment. Your imagination will lead you to other ways to symbolically bring families into the classroom and emphasize their lasting value to the school.

Chapter IV
Extending Classroom Experiences:
Ongoing Activities for At-Home Parent Engagement

"She's gonna love this, Mom! Remember, her daughter lives in Australia!"

Samantha certainly remembered the unit we developed about Australia. She had researched koalas with her mom and reported the sleeping and eating habits of the adorable teddy bear-like creatures to the class during circle time. She even published her research findings in our Australia research binder, where more than thirty pages of research from other families was compiled.

What made the greatest impression on Samantha, however, was the personal connection she made when my daughter (who, yes, lives in Australia) visited the classroom. When Samantha was a first grader in another classroom, she was on a walk with her mom and found a boomerang-shaped rock. They agreed Samantha would wash it, dry it, paint it, and place it on my desk to surprise me. When she was a student in my class, she would often leave me small gifts.

I began my teaching career more than twenty years ago in a public school that had always implemented an "open door" policy with parents. It wasn't unusual to enter my classroom and see two or three parents volunteering most days of the week. Relationships were built through volunteerism, face-to-face interactions at morning drop-off and afternoon pick-up, and the occasional, "I was in the neighborhood and had a few minutes and thought I'd stop in" moment.

I grew very comfortable with the fluidity of my parent relationships. I'd gather information about Tristan, who spent the night at Grandma's house; Hillary, who didn't sleep well the night before; or Joseph, who was feeling anxious about a dental appointment. These and a myriad of other personal stories were delivered directly from parents who stood in my classroom doorway.

Unfortunately, the Sandy Hook tragedy of December 2012 changed the manner in which elementary schools conduct business. Security systems were installed, safety procedures were implemented, and my "open doors" were closed. This didn't diminish my resolve to build relationships with families. My commitment remained steadfast and, in fact, even grew in strength.

I've always believed that the pathway for global wellness lies in the spirit of children who deserve to be cared for by communities of adults with a common goal and purpose: to raise healthy and compassionate children. I believe in the proverb, "It takes a village to raise a child."

When my school's new security measures kept me from seeing parents regularly, I realized I had to find new ways to reach out. As a result, I decided to use a number of activities to build parent engagement through what I call the Confetti Approach. Just as people throw confetti by the handful, never quite knowing where it will land, I make these activities available to all parents, never quite knowing which parents will decide to participate.

My approach is intended to create different avenues of activity that match the interests, talents, resources, and schedules of busy working parents with whom I wish to build villages by creating different open doors. My purpose is to make sure those walls that were constructed to ensure safety do not separate teachers from the families they serve. Just as we differentiate our instruction for children based upon need, it is my intention to differentiate opportunities for involvement.

Many parents would like to spend more time volunteering in their children's classrooms; the reality is that a large number of parents work and have overtaxed schedules and stretched resources. Taking a morning off to volunteer in a classroom is a luxury, not the norm. The at-home activities in this chapter are designed with those parents in mind.

Not every activity will appeal to every parent or guardian, but it only takes one activity, or piece of confetti, to catch an adult's interest. Meaningful parent-child interactions will follow. Don't worry about keeping track of which parent participates in which activity. My strategies to involve families are numerous, and tracking them would require energies that are better spent developing relationships. The activity itself is not as important as the opportunity to create an extension of the classroom in which parents and children can interact through learning experiences at home.

Many of the following activities are not new but are long-standing effective strategies for delivering curriculum. What *is* new is the intention to deliberately engage parents in the activities. Instead of adding yet another thing to my plate, I looked at the activities I already implemented in my classroom and simply considered how I could expand them to include parents.

These activities empower parents to be active participants in their children's educational experiences, even if they aren't able to step into the classroom. Empowered parents foster eager learners. Engaged parents support teachers and their children's learning environment which nurtures parents, children, teachers, and the community. Maria Montessori wrote:

> The first phase of the child's development goes from birth to, let us say, six years of age. At this stage the child is partly at home, partly in school. ... education should take both the situations into consideration. (1971, p. 2)

Keep tossing the confetti opportunities; you just never know which one may stick. Enough confetti can build a village!

Cooking: Sharing Classroom Recipes to Recreate at Home

Each day, 31 three-to-six year-old children enter our Montessori classroom. They hang backpacks on their hooks, place their lunchboxes in baskets, and then descend upon the circle time area with stories and treasures from home to share. They are happy to see their friends and are full of questions about all sorts of things, including the activities planned for the day. It's typically a joyful bustle of activity and the jubilant din reflects it. We gather around the circle and begin our day with songs, books, and lessons.

Twice a month, on Thursday mornings, the cooking folder accompanies me to the circle. The clamor on those Thursdays is a little more enthusiastic because, "It's cooking day!"

I am fortunate to have a couple of parents who volunteer in my classroom for the purposes of cooking with a small group of children. (See Chapter V, *Classroom Volunteerism*, p. 77, for more details on classroom cooking with volunteers.)

On the first cooking day of the school year, I tell the children that three or four of them will be invited to cook on each cooking day. If they wish to participate in cooking they say, "Yes, please." They will be invited another time if they say, "No, thank you."

Those children who participate have their names recorded in the cooking folder along with the date they cook. Once every child has had the chance to participate, children may be invited to participate a second time. The children, referred to as our "cooking friends," accompany our cooking volunteer to the teachers' break room where the recipe, ingredients, and cooking materials are available.

The volunteer and children work together to prepare the dish. They wash, cut, measure, and mix the ingredients together. They set timers, sweep the floor, and wash the dishes. Finally, they present the food they have made to the rest of the class.

Cooking friends serve their classmates

At the appropriate time, the cooking friends ring the classroom bell and announce that the "tasting" is ready. We gather at the circle area.

The cooking friends ask the other children, "Would you like to taste (name of dish)?"

The children respond with "Yes, please." or "No, thank you."

Children who especially enjoy the tasting experience are generally the last to leave the group, and they often ask for a second taste! This provides the opportunity for discussion. I invite those children to tell mom or dad or a grown-up about the recipe they tasted and ask their parents to help them make the recipe at home and share the tasting experience.

In this way, a scrumptious dish tasted at school can become the catalyst for a meaningful child-adult interaction and can bring parents into the collaborative learning circle. Food plays an important role in building community. Think about family gatherings or other social events you've attended—people always seem to congregate around the food! As children prepare food for one another in the classroom, they build community. And they expand on that community when they make the recipe again at home.

I share the recipes with parents in my weekly newsletter, or post them on our class website. I also always include a few "greatest hits" recipes that have been successful in my classroom time and again. Below is a note to parents that I include in every newsletter that accompanies a classroom recipe.

> Cooking is a wonderful way to practice learning skills at home — and it's delicious too! Food preparation demonstrates cause and effect relationships, reinforces sequencing, promotes higher-level thinking skills, exercises problem solving, fosters independence, and involves all the senses in a tasty, powerful, and memorable learning experience. Please ask your child how they liked the following recipe when we made it in class. If it was a hit, try it at home!

Fruit Smoothies
    1 quart strawberries, hulled
    1 banana, peeled
    2 peaches, pitted and sliced
    1 cup mango juice
    2 cups ice cubes

In a blender, combine strawberries, banana, and peaches. Blend until fruit is pureed. Blend in the juice. Add ice and blend to desired consistency. Pour into glasses, serve, and enjoy!

Ice Cream in a Bag
    ½ cup whole milk
    ½ teaspoon vanilla
    1 tablespoon sugar
    4 cups crushed ice
    4 tablespoons salt

Special equipment:
    1 quart-size zipper plastic bag
    1 gallon-size zipper plastic freezer bag
    Mittens or gloves

Combine milk, vanilla, and sugar in the quart-size bag. Seal tightly. Place ice and salt in the gallon-size bag. Place the quart-size bag into the gallon-size bag and seal. Put on your mittens and begin shaking the bags. Continue to shake until the ice cream is firm to the touch. (It should have the consistency of soft-serve ice cream). Lift the quart bag from the gallon bag and wipe it to remove as much salt as possible. Pour the soft-serve ice cream into a bowl or eat it directly from the bag!

Crockpot Applesauce

> 3 pounds apples, peeled, cored,
> and sliced
> ½ cup packed brown sugar
> 1½ tablespoons lemon juice
> 1 teaspoon ground cinnamon

In a slow cooker, combine the apples, brown sugar, and lemon juice. Cook on high for three to four hours. Mash with a potato masher into the consistency you desire. Stir in cinnamon. You can serve this hot, at room temperature, or cold. It is great over vanilla ice cream!

Homemade Butter

> Heavy whipping cream
> A jar with a lid
> A grown-up or friend to help shake
> the jar when your child gets tired

Pour the whipping cream into a jar, filling it about one-quarter of the way. Screw the lid on the jar tightly. Begin to shake the jar. Continue to shake until the cream thickens and butter starts to form. A liquid called buttermilk will separate from the cream and surround the butter. Pour off the buttermilk and spread the butter onto a cracker or bread. Our classroom friends like to spread the butter onto toast and sprinkle it with cinnamon and sugar for a special treat!

What Are the Benefits of Cooking Activities and Sending Recipes Home?

The students' enthusiasm for cooking is contagious, and the time we set aside for this activity does more than engage them. It provides students with the life skills of preparation, cleanup, and serving a meal, and lets them practice the grace and courtesy skills of formal dining. Cooking experiences integrate science, math, social studies, and language activities into early childhood and elementary classrooms.

For years, parents have been delighted to have these classroom cooking activities translated to home, especially if they are unable to volunteer in the classroom during the day. One student, Grace, took home her weekly newsletter with the Homemade Butter recipe. Grace's mother responded to her excitement, and they successfully made the recipe at home. Grace followed up the experience by making homemade butter for their seven guests at Thanksgiving dinner! She and her family members shook individual baby food-sized jars of heavy cream; one jar of the finished butter graced each place setting. Through this activity, Grace's family embraced the opportunity to extend learning into their home.

After the holiday, Grace and her mother eagerly shared their story with me; throughout the year they continued to tell me of their successes in repeating school recipes or activities at home. The connection we built paid off; later that year I had to discuss a classroom concern with Grace's parents. There was already a well-established, positive relationship in place, and one could say we approached the issue with the "smoothness of butter."

Instead of each of us expecting the other to fix the problem, we developed a plan to work together to help Grace be successful at school. It was so helpful to have already built a relationship based on cooperation.

Grace's and her mother's overt enthusiasm and communication about their recipe successes is not always the norm. More often, I hear of recipes made at home in a passing conversation with a student or parent. For example, one day, three-year-old Randall reported to me, "My daddy likes snowball cookies!" We had made this treat in January. It cheers me to think that families might still be making snowball cookies in May. Even if I don't hear about every recipe when it is made at home, these experiences continue to provide a way for parents to feel connected to the school.

Variations on this Activity

In addition to the child-tested and approved recipes above, I also like to use recipes that could work for holidays and special occasions—times when families often cook together. I enjoy recipes from around the world because I can work them in with geography or cultural lessons. I also enjoy recipes derived from or inspired by literature, such as Chicken Soup with Rice (based on Maurice Sendak's book of the same name) or Stone Soup (based on Jon J. Muth's version of the folktale). Finally, edible science experiments, like demonstrating the three states of matter while working with gelatin, are always popular!

Sharing: Themed Show-and-Tell Experiences

Treasures for show-and-tell make their way to school in many shapes, sizes, colors, and forms. They may be unique works of art or craftsmanship. Some whistle, some beep, and some even glow in the dark. They do share one common characteristic, however: they all come from home in the hands of a proud child. When it comes to show-and-tell, you won't have to encourage excitement in your students—show-and-tell never gets old to them.

You can impart even more enthusiasm by including families in the process of choosing beloved items to share. This activity can be even more meaningful when it is linked to a classroom theme, giving parents windows into what their children are learning.

On the second Tuesday of each month, we have a color-themed "Sharing Day." While our sharing might sometimes focus on things such as shapes or natural objects, the second Tuesday focuses on the "color of the month," which is also linked to a "trait of the month." I find that the color becomes a cue to help students remember the trait.

For example, the color could be *indigo*, and the trait could be *faith*. I let families know about the themed sharing in advance by noting it in our weekly and monthly newsletters.

Indigo Sharing Day: January 29

The character trait for January is **Faith** and is assigned the color **Indigo**.

Faith is the quality that reminds us to believe in things that are not evident. We have faith in ourselves, in our abilities, and in our potential. As parents and teachers, we believe in our children and in the choices we make for them. Together, we guide and help children reach their highest potential. Children make great leaps of faith each day as they try new things and make new discoveries.

We'll celebrate *Faith* with an *Indigo* Sharing Day on January 29! Wear something dark blue or bring something indigo to school to share!

Consistency is helpful in achieving parent participation—having the color-themed sharing day on the second Tuesday of the month creates a rhythm to our classroom calendar that parents can easily anticipate. I chose Tuesday because it gives me a chance to remind children on Monday of the sharing day, rather than having a Monday event that could easily be forgotten over the weekend.

The Indigo Gallery

I bring up the sharing at Monday's circle time. "This note on our calendar reminds me that tomorrow is *Indigo Sharing Day*. Ask Mom or Dad or a grown-up at home to help you find an object that is indigo."

This reminder builds excitement for the next day's sharing.

The next morning, Aanya, whom I affectionately refer to as "joy with feet," triumphantly announces her arrival with her mother's indigo scarf. She's been talking about this scarf since last week, so I know her mother has been involved with the decision and is allowing her to bring it to school.

I invite a child to place a small rug on the floor. On it I place an index card that reads *indigo*. The beloved items will be displayed here and admired for the day. The children enter the circle time area wearing various shades of blue. Backpacks and bags are rattling, and young voices are chattering. It's always so difficult to wait to show such wonderful treasures!

Once the children are seated around the circle, we begin. One by one, the children stand and share their *indigo* items. They usually talk about where they found their items and why they like them. If they don't have much to say, I offer gentle prompts: "Did someone at home help you find it?" When a child has finished, they place their item on the rug, and the next child has a turn. When everyone has shared, the children are reminded that our gallery is for observing and admiring our friends' sharing, and that we look at the items with hands held behind our backs. Our Indigo Gallery remains in our classroom for the day, and at the end of the day, the items go home in backpacks.

Whether its *indigo* sharing day or any other sharing day, if a child comes to class empty-handed, I ask, "Bobby, did you have something to share with us today?"

If the child says "No", I always respond with, "That's okay. Would you like to bring your leaf (color, shape, etc.) another day?" Often the child returns the next day with the theme-based sharing. If not, I let it go—this child will have many other opportunities to participate.

What Are the Benefits of Themed Sharing?

This work is beneficial to the children in a number of ways: it reinforces concepts and contextual vocabulary; it gives children opportunities to compare, contrast, and classify items; and it builds community, as children dress in similar colors on a particular day. When deciding on an item to bring from home, children have the opportunity to partner with a parent or other adult to connect classroom content (in this case, color) to daily experiences, develop oral language, and work on creative expression. Those opportunities are repeated when they present their item to their classmates.

This activity is just as helpful for connecting with parents. It informs and includes them in the development of classroom themes and offers a natural entry point for a family discussion about the trait the color represents. Even choosing the word "indigo" over the words "dark blue" serves a purpose; family members' ears perk up when they hear requests such as,

- "Mommy, is this block indigo?"
- "Daddy, which crayon looks indigo to you?"
- "Grandpa, can I take your indigo tie to school?"

They think, "Wow, my child knows the word indigo."

This is no small accomplishment. Awakening families' curiosity about their children's school lives can nudge them to learn more about what's happening in school. And they may want to get involved! For example, one day my student Jade passed along a message from her mother, who wondered if we would have a violet sharing day sometime since violet was her favorite color. My response was an overwhelming, "Yes!" What a gift to have a parent so invested in the sharing.

Variations on this Activity

I love our color/character trait themed sharing. Themed sharing can relate to any of the topics your class is exploring and will transmit a message to families about what the children are currently learning. A leaf-sharing day in October is a strong indicator that a fall unit is in development. Finding a leaf on an autumn day can be done quickly on the way to school and provides parents and children with a reason to stop and together enjoy the beauty of fall colors. Sometimes we all need a reminder to slow down our busy lives and smell the roses—or gather the leaves, as it were!

A few other themes that have been successful in my classroom include:

- letters or sounds
- seasonal natural items such as leaves, pumpkins, or flowers
- timeless natural items such as rocks and seashells
- family or pet photographs
- items relating to sports, activities, or transportation
- opposites (rough/smooth, large/small, heavy/light)
- books by certain authors (such as Dr. Seuss or Eric Carle)

Earth Day Sharing

No matter what theme you choose, the communication you send home before the sharing gives you an opportunity to introduce families to the concepts you're addressing in class and the terms you'll be using with students. For example, the following announcement about Circle and Square Sharing Day emphasizes that these shapes are flat, not three-dimensional.

Circle and Square Sharing Day

On Tuesday, August 26, we will have a group sharing experience.

All our friends are invited to find a circle or a square to share with all their other friends during Tuesday morning sharing.

Circles are flat shapes that can be cut from paper or found at home.

Squares are flat shapes that can be cut from paper or found at home.

Circles and Squares should be small enough to fit in children's backpacks so they can be safely transported.

A Home-to-School Ambassador:
"Bud the Bear" Gives Each Child's Family a Voice in Our Classroom

In her book *To Educate the Human Potential,* Maria Montessori noted the importance of interconnection:

> We shall walk together on this path of life, for all things are part of the universe and are connected with each other to form one whole unity. (1948, p. 8)

Many of my classroom activities touch the minds and hearts of children and parents, but one of the most popular and well-received is "Bud the Bear." Bud is a stuffed teddy bear with a threadbare nose, fur that has been loved into something that is less than plush, and floppy joints from lots of flips and many walks in the hands of delighted children who have the chance to bring Bud home. Bud connects every family to every other student in my classroom.

"Jessica brought Bud back, Mrs. Harman! Today's the day I'm going to get to take him to my house!" Randall is the youngest child in my class and has been developing such patience as he awaits his turn to host Bud.

"Maybe, Randall. We'll see whose name Jessica pulls from the sack. If it's not your name this time, it's okay. Your name is still in the sack and someday a friend will choose the paper with your name on it."

Jessica has just returned Bud the Bear to the classroom. She proudly swings Bud in his canvas traveling bag; his tattered ears and beady plastic eyes peek out. Jessica's body language speaks volumes. She struts to the circle area with an enormous grin, taking the longest possible route through the classroom, just in case someone hasn't noticed that Bud the Bear is back and that she has been the child in charge of his care. She sits down with the group, removes Bud from his bag, and places him in a place of honor upon her lap. She lifts his journal (an ordinary composition book on which I've taped a photo of Bud and a label that reads "Bud's Journal 2017-2018). She proudly places it on the floor in front of her and waits for everyone's attention, grinning all the while.

"Did you have a nice visit?" I ask.

Somehow, the grin gets broader!

To help children and their families envision what a visit with Bud might include and what a journal entry might look like, I write a letter of introduction in the front of Bud's journal.

> Hello, my friends. My name is Bud the Bear. I live in Mrs. Harman's classroom, but I love to go to new places and meet new friends. All my friends will have a chance to take me home overnight. I'll bring my carrying bag and my journal with me. Please take a picture of me visiting your home or doing something special with you. If you don't have a printer at your home, please let Mrs. Harman know so she can take our picture together at school. I've had my picture taken with grandparents, and at piano lessons, soccer games and even birthday parties! Or you may draw a picture instead of taking a photograph.
>
> Don't forget to leave some room on your journal page for the image! When you are done journaling, drawing, or gluing down your picture, bring me, my journal, and my bag back to school. Mrs. Harman will read to all our friends about our visit. Please keep me for only three or four days, since I have many friends to visit. Thank you for taking such good care of me!
>
> Love,
> Bud the Bear

To help get families started, I also write the first journal entry. I am a breast cancer survivor, and I make it a habit to bring Bud with me to our yearly Susan G. Komen Race for the Cure. My family and I always take a photo with him at the event. My entry models a format that other families can follow, and it lets them know that the journal is a place where they can share meaningful aspects of their own lives, which will be honored by the classroom community.

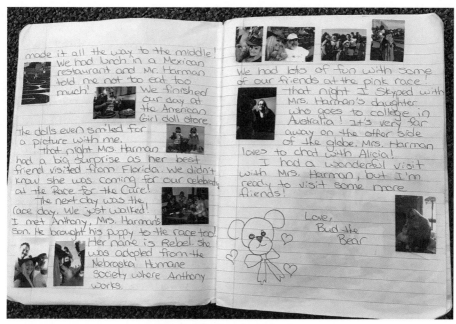

My Bud the Bear journal entry

The other children arrive, and we begin our show-and-tell while awaiting morning announcements over the loudspeaker. Once we're all seated around our circle, I ask Jessica if she is ready to share Bud the Bear. She and Bud scoot over to sit directly in front of me. She hands me the journal, and I leaf through the many pages filled with adult handwriting, printed pictures, and children's artwork of Bud from the other families that Bud has visited this year.

But today is Jessica's moment to shine. Jessica's pages are easy to find—her parents have taped several pictures of her and Bud into the journal. I hold up the journal as I would any other children's book, with the pages facing the children. I read out loud what Jessica's parents have handwritten about Bud's inclusion in family activities, like dinner and bedtime routines. Jessica interrupts, too excited for me to read on, to tell about the bed she made for Bud and the other teddy bears he met at her home. Mostly she wants to talk about the pictures that her mom and dad took of her while Bud was with their family. I return the journal to Bud's bag, and Jessica follows with Bud, nestling him in securely.

Now it's time to determine the next host. Jessica pulls a little slip of paper from the sack of names. She reads Randall's name aloud. "Yay, it's me! I knew it!"

Randall's joy reverberates through my classroom—and probably through the classrooms to the north and south as well. Randall was right; it was his day to take Bud home! The visit will be a tremendous success, and Bud the Bear will return, snuggled in a luxurious velveteen quilt made by Randall's grandma.

Not every visit ends with Bud receiving a gift like that quilt, and not every journal entry includes pages of details or photos. However, every visit is met with enthusiasm from every student and family. Even Nhi, whose parents did not speak English, ensured that Bud had an entry after visiting their family: they enlisted an older sibling to write in Bud's journal. The effort spoke volumes!

One of the many benefits of a Montessori classroom is that it is multi-age. As a result, many children spend more than one year with me. Bud and I have the privilege of watching siblings and families grow on the pages of his journal. And children in their second or third year with me know Bud the Bear will be a part of our classroom activities—his initial arrival at the beginning of the school year is a highly anticipated event. I also set the stage for his appearance by building a bear literary unit around him, sharing books such as *Corduroy* by Don Freeman and Frank Asch's books about bears.

Any type of stuffed animal may work as a "home-to-school ambassador." I like to give the ambassador a three-letter phonetic name that's simple for children to read and write: Tim, Bob, Dot, Sam, Mac, Meg, and Max are just a few examples. It can help to choose a name based on the animal you have—for example, Bud the Bear, Max the Moose, Tim the Turtle, Dot the Dinosaur.

I find the most important quality in an ambassador is its potential for being loved by a child while still surviving its travels. In Margery Williams's *The Velveteen Rabbit*, the Skin Horse explains how to become real:

… it doesn't happen often to people who break easily, or have sharp edges, or who have to be carefully kept. Generally, by the time you are Real, most of your hair has been loved off, and your eyes drop out and you get loose in your joints and very shabby. (1922, p. 16)

Bud has become as worn as the Velveteen Rabbit himself, but the children never seem to notice any shabbiness.

Sharing Bud's latest journal entry with the class

A page from Bud the Bear's Journal

Each year, Bud quickly becomes an integral part of our classroom community. At the end of each school year, as a gift for the students and as a reminder of their time in our community, I take a picture of each child holding Bud. Then I laminate the photos and attach magnets to them. I've attended at least five high school graduation parties where I've seen these magnets. Some refrigerator doors display three of them, one for each year the child spent in my class.

What Are the Benefits of a Home-to-School Ambassador?

Bud has been traveling to the homes of my students for nearly twenty years, with 100% parent participation. He travels with a new journal each year and is working on his second carrying bag, which is now collecting patches from his travels. He has an extensive wardrobe courtesy of generous parents and baby siblings, a lovely denim quilt made by an enthralled grandmother, and even a bear-sized guitar signed by the star of a reality TV show! The power in these stories is not the swag that Bud has accumulated; rather, it's the energy that families have put into the project.

Bud the Bear gives families the rare opportunity to introduce themselves, in their own words, to our class. Bud serves as a powerful tool for connection and is much more than a tattered old stuffed animal. The journal travels from family to family. As families get a chance to know each other, they articulate unique ideas, information, and vocabulary, such as names of family members and pets, parents' professions, and favorite destinations. Familial cultures, experiences, and customs are recorded, and meals, significant events, and spiritual traditions are also shared. The photographs provide glimpses into homes and routines. Each family shares a bit about themselves with our entire classroom community in Bud's journal.

The well-worn traveling bear and his journal also provide parents with the opportunity to work with their children on literacy skills—reading, listening, and writing about something that has happened. Collectively, the families in my classroom are recording a period of time in history, from the moment Bud leaves school until his return several days later.

Often, it's difficult to tell who enjoys the experiences with Bud more—the parents or the child! The three or four days that Bud spends in a family's home give them all a connection that lasts far longer. If parents of former students spot me at the grocery store, they may not remember my name, but they often ask, "Aren't you the teacher with Bud the Bear?"

Everything about their experience with Bud is positive: their child's excitement about bringing him home, their family's contribution to Bud's journal, the feeling that Bud is someone they know. Being able to reference Bud's visit when I talk to a parent is like discovering that the two of us have a mutual beloved friend. Families that have not yet hosted Bud have often heard of him and eagerly anticipate his visit. Even when I am contacting a family with a concern about a student or when I am wrapping up a serious parent conference, a mention of Bud's upcoming visit to their home or a comment about how much Bud seemed to enjoy his visit with them, helps them to remember we are all part of the same classroom family.

Wish Lists

My mother used to tell me, "Honey, I can't help you if I don't know what you need."

She was quite right. The same is true for classroom needs. Parents are often very willing to contribute needed classroom materials, from empty toilet paper tubes to gift cards. And, like my mom, they're happy—even relieved to help. We just have to let them know what we need.

My favorite scene from the holiday film classic *A Christmas Story* is when Ralphie, the lead character, approaches his teacher carrying a fruit basket that is so large you can't actually see him (you can only see his hands grasping the basket in front of him). My student Dillon had that same experience as he staggered into class with a bag of cockatiel food for our classroom pet, Willow. It appeared the bag was walking into my room of its own accord (on Dillon's red cowboy boots). A muffled voice from somewhere behind the bag said, "Here you go, Mrs. Harman. My mom and I bought this for Willow."

Dillon's mother is a wonderfully generous person with a special place in her heart for animals. Because she is a working mom, she can't volunteer regularly in our classroom. She keeps informed of our classroom needs via my weekly newsletter (in particular a section titled "Classroom Donations"). Here's an example:

> Occasionally our friends and families like to make donations to our classroom. Those donations could include:
>
> - empty toilet paper tubes
> - gently used single mittens for mitten washing
> - liquid soap
> - colorful buttons
> - goldfish food

Not every newsletter includes a wish list. I also vary the amount of time between when I ask for something and when I need it depending on the specificity of the item: if I'm looking for short, wide-mouthed glass jars, it may take more time to collect them than if I ask for toilet-paper tubes, which every family can provide. I try to include donations that don't require anything to be purchased—toilet paper or paper towel tubes, packing peanuts, jigsaw puzzle pieces, milk jug caps, fabric or ribbon scraps, etc. Some families, however, are able and want to buy things for the classroom, so I periodically ask for those items as well: food for classroom pets, markers and other art media, and specific materials like replacement pegs for pegboards.

I'll tell you a secret: I don't share a wish list with parents because I cannot obtain these items. As my husband will attest, I am continually building my own supply of short, wide-mouthed glass jars, and I will go to the pet store to get fish food if we need it. I ask for these items because it gives parents another way to feel connected to what is going on in our classroom, no matter what their schedules are. We *do* use the materials that are donated, and that is a wonderful benefit of this activity. If my donation requests don't result in all the materials I need, I'll make up the difference myself.

This activity doesn't require any extra time to introduce—my only communication with parents is via the newsletter. Yet, when I give families specific, manageable requests, donations magically appear over the next few days or weeks. One morning, Noah was extremely amused as he pulled a bag of empty toilet paper tubes from his backpack: "Don't ask me why my mom put THESE in my backpack!"

Noah's parents read my newsletter, so they knew that we were going to make shakers with the tubes (as a preparation for an upcoming field trip to the symphony). In addition to amusement, you may notice expressions of pride and happiness upon the faces of your Dillons, Noahs, and Ralphies as they bring donations to you!

My students often like to bring their donations to share at our morning circle time, even though it's not required. They enjoy showing the class what they have brought for our community, and it often sparks conversation. Another option is a dedicated "donation basket" in the classroom where students can leave their gifts.

I respond to all donations with a thank you note accompanying the parent's individual weekly newsletter. These donations are truly gifts, and they deserve to be treated as such—not to mention that I now have one more opportunity for connection with students' families.

> Dear (child's name) and family,
>
> Your donation to our classroom is deeply appreciated. Thank you for your generosity and participation in our classroom wish-list activity!
>
> Sincerely,
> Mrs. Harman

What Are the Benefits of Giving Families a Wish List?

Donating or purchasing materials for the classroom allows parents to participate in an indirect, yet powerful, way. It feels good, too. Research conducted by Harvard Business School (Anik et al, 2009) suggests that charitable giving can create an improved sense of well-being and helps inform the giver about the organization receiving the gift.

Regardless of the value of the gift or the procedures you develop, your classroom, children, and parents will benefit from the opportunity to share with others. You may even help develop a spirit of giving in your children, which could become a way of life!

As with many of the other confetti activities in this chapter, giving families a wish list gives them an opportunity to contribute at whatever level they are able. Many parents' schedules prevent them from being able to visit the classroom, but they are able and willing to add a small item to their grocery list, or remember to save some recyclable items to bring in from home. I am equally grateful for all of them. I remember this quote by L. O. Baird, "May no gift be too small to give nor too simple to receive which is wrapped in thoughtfulness and tied with love."

Variations on this Activity

If holiday gift-giving is common in your classroom, you may want to provide families with a gift card wish list, which they can use in lieu of personal gifts to you.

> Each holiday season we are blessed by the generosity of our families. Although your kindness is deeply appreciated, we would like you to consider making a gift card donation to our classroom instead of personal gifts. Those donations could include:
>
> - teacher store gift cards
>   (Learning Station, Lakeshore)
> - bookstore gift cards
> - office supply store gift cards
> - craft store gift cards

Wish lists don't need to be confined to a single classroom. My school's Parent Teacher Organization posts a "giving tree" bulletin board outside the school entrance. The paper tree is filled with die-cut apples; on each apple is written a material needed with the teacher's name. The apples are color-coded by teacher so parents can easily locate their teacher's apples.

Sound Bags: Engaging Parents in a Phonemic Awareness Activity

We first learn to read with our ears.

This may seem like an odd statement, but I find myself repeating it year after year during parent-teacher conferences. I explain that prior to formal reading, children must acquire phonemic awareness skills: the ability to manipulate and isolate sounds.

Sound bags are a language activity that I have integrated into my Montessori classroom and are easily extended from school to home. Children and parents work together to gather objects that have a common initial (beginning) sound. This activity has a dual benefit: students get to share pieces of their home lives with their classmates, and parents get to be involved in our classroom curriculum.

"Mrs. Harman, I brought my sound bag back today. I bet you can't guess what is in it," says Emily as she squeezes the drawstring bag.

Its contents are bulging, and a distinctive electronic "meow" emanates from the bag as she hugs it tight. Emily proudly sits at our circle time with the bag on her lap. She's eager for her friends to arrive. When everyone is seated, Emily opens the bag and removes and names aloud an electronic "cat" (that obligingly meows), a "car", and a "card". Nearly every child raises their hand to name the beginning sound the objects have in common. Emily calls upon Tristyn, who announces to the class that the objects begin with the sound /k/ (hard "c").

Emily announces, "You're right!" and smiles at Tristyn to acknowledge his cleverness.

She then returns her objects to her cubby to take home and hangs the sound bag on one of the four sound bag hooks in the classroom, ready for the next child.

Each of my students will have multiple opportunities to fill a sound bag during the year while they work through the entire alphabet, building their initial sound skills at their own pace. Sound bags connect the work that the children are doing in school: tracing the Montessori sandpaper letters; generating a verbal list of items that began with a certain sound (such as cake, corn, candy, and candles); and tracking the sounds they have learned in their "sound books."

Each sound bag holds a note that explains the process of finding objects to fill the bag for our sound guessing activity. It describes how to isolate initial sounds and invites adults to participate.

The laminated note has blanks for the individual sound, which I fill in with a dry-erase marker.

> I am bringing home a sound bag. Today I learned the sound _/k/_. Please help me find objects that begin with the sound _/k/_ like in the word _cat_. Please help me place the objects in the bag and return the bag with the objects to school. I'll share my objects with my friends, and they will try to guess my sound. At the end of the day, I'll bring my objects home.

This note explains the activity well, but before each family receives it, I'll have given them other introductions to it. During a curriculum meeting early in the year, I bring up the idea of sound bags, and I discuss them in a newsletter as well. That way, when the bag arrives at home, families are ready. During the curriculum meeting, I explain the process of using sound bags and demonstrate how children present their bags during circle time, so adults can better understand what the activity requires of children.

At the parent meeting, I like to fill my sound bag with a plastic slice of watermelon, a wagon, and a wheel. I begin the meeting by slowly withdrawing and pronouncing the name of each object, (with a bit of flair and drama for added fun). I ask for a volunteer to share the *sound* (not the letter) heard at the beginning of each word. If a parent shares the letter name, I acknowledge the letter name and guide the parent from the name to the sound of the letter. I explain that adults can participate in two ways—they can assist their children in finding the objects, or they can review the objects to be certain the sound listed on the note is indeed the initial (beginning) sound of the objects found in the bag.

What Are the Benefits of Engaging Parents in Phonemic Awareness Activities with Sound Bags?

According to research by Cotton and Wikelund:

> The most effective forms of parent involvement are those which engage parents in working directly with their children on learning activities at home. (1989, p. 3)

Sound bags give families an opportunity to engage with children's development of phonemic awareness, which is "… the best predictor of the ease of early reading acquisition, better even than IQ, vocabulary, and listening comprehension." (Sensenbaugh, 1996)

Having the opportunity to reinforce a school skill at home empowers parents and makes them feel acknowledged as valuable co-teachers.

This activity also prepares parents for the homework assignments that await their children in the coming years at school. It provides parents an opportunity to discuss with their children what they are learning at school; it introduces parents to how classroom norms inform the expectations for homework (in this case, adults learn that the work is about the sound, not the letter); and it presents "homework" as an exercise that families can support.

This experience sets the tone for future positive experiences with homework. I often hear from parents that this activity has given their children a powerful "aha" moment that motivates them to direct their own learning. Parents witness their children becoming experts at this activity and watch as their children derive internal rewards for their efforts. I've heard stories of children excitedly trying to fill their bags as much as they possibly can and giddily rehearsing with their parents how they will present their findings in class the next day.

Children exercise their learning skills at home, and their family's involvement tells them these skills are important. And, this learning takes place within a framework of fun—searching for objects or treasures at home.

Variations on this Activity

Initial sounds need not be limited to the twenty-six letters of the alphabet. Digraphs such as *sh*, *th*, and *ch*, or long vowel diphthongs such as *ee*, *oa*, and *ai*, can be mixed in with the twenty-six single sounds if it is more appropriate for the child's abilities or if the sound bag is such a popular activity that the children need additional challenge.

Living History: Sharing Birthday Timelines

Children love to look at their baby pictures. Quite frankly, who doesn't enjoy reminiscing while poring over old photographs? The nostalgia this engenders may be psychologically and physiologically beneficial, helping us build bonds with those around us (Weller, 2013). In my classroom, our Birthday Timelines combine these benefits while also forging a deep connection with parents.

Pari arrives at school in a fluffy lavender dress with a matching sweater and patent leather shoes. She glides into the classroom with a twirl and something that resembles a curtsy. "It's my birthday! I'm five now. My mommy's bringing cupcakes. I have princess rings. Here's my timeline."

She hands me a manila envelope. Inside are several sheets of standard copy machine paper that have been adorned with photographic and narrative chronicles of her developmental changes over the five years of her life. Pari takes a breath and begins her day, anticipating her classroom birthday celebration later that afternoon.

Pari and her family have been hard at work creating the timeline that she is waiting to present. Each page is devoted to a year of her life and is filled with pictures, notes, and stories about Pari and her life's milestones—first words, first steps, favorite foods, toys, and places visited. When creating these timelines, parents and children alike become deeply engaged as they select just the right pictures to include.

I introduce the birthday timelines in a newsletter at the beginning of each school year:

Birthday Celebration Timelines

We celebrate birthdays (and half-birthdays for friends with summer birthdays) by walking around our circle area while carrying a model of Earth. We orbit the Sun (the birthday candle represents our Sun) once for each year of the child's life. Parents are welcome to join us for our celebrations, which generally occur at 2:45, but please check with us to confirm the time.

Children are invited to bring a Personal Timeline as part of their birthday celebration. A photograph or several photographs along with a narrative of each year of your child's life — likes/dislikes, developmental milestones (walking, talking), birth of siblings, early school experiences — chronicle your child's life and are an important part of our history curriculum. A packet will be sent home several weeks prior to your child's birthday with a page for each year of your child's life. Please add photographs and milestone information that will be shared at your child's birthday celebration.

The same note is included in the packet I send home several weeks prior to the child's birthday. It also includes sheets of paper with the headings "1 Year," "2 Years," "3 Years," "4 Years," "5 Years," etc. Some parents will attach the photographs and narratives directly to those pages; others will use the headings as guidelines as they create more elaborate scrapbook pages.

When we celebrate Pari's birthday at the end of the day, her mother joins us. Pari and her mother show her classmates her timeline, read it aloud, and point to photographs. Timelines make birthdays a celebration of an individual's life, and they provide opportunities to contemplate the passage of time from the past to the present. The children enjoy the cupcakes that Pari's mother brings to the celebration, but in my experience, having her mother present and reflecting on her entire life with her classroom friends is likely more important to Pari than any confection.

Child's timeline

What Are the Benefits of Involving Parents with Birthday Timelines?

This activity is powerful because children who observe others' timelines get glimpses into familial traditions that may differ from theirs. Children observe similarities in child development and begin to understand the chronology of their own lives. For me, though, the most remarkable aspect of this activity is how it honors and welcomes parents.

The birthday celebrations in our class give parents an opportunity to share their love for their child, both when creating the timeline and when they share part of the special day with their child and the class as a whole. The time parents and children spend together looking through photographs and talking about childhood milestones must be pretty special as well (most children and parents beam when the timeline is read aloud).

McAlister's mom so enjoyed making his timeline that she told me she intends "to make a new page for each of his years and will present it to him as a high school graduation gift."

What a terrific gift that began in an early childhood classroom!

Moreover, timelines communicate respect for parents. Although children spend a great deal of time under our guidance, their first and most important teachers are their parents. Engaging parents to help create the timeline affirms their expert knowledge of their child and their vital role as a parent. This work also lets parents know that you and the other children in the class value their child. Could there be a better way to establish and strengthen trust with a parent?

A Variation on this Activity

I've had several students in my classroom over the length of my career who did not celebrate birthdays, but whose parents chose to share personal timelines nonetheless. This activity looks exactly the same as a birthday timeline with milestones and memories of each year, but it is presented as a "history timeline" of the child instead of a birthday timeline. The intention is the same—it is about honoring children and parents—and it doesn't have to be tied to a birthday.

Home as a Data Source: Building Graphing Skills

- "I did my homework."
- "How many plants do you have?"
- "That's more than I have."
- "My dad helped me count my plants."

These are snippets of conversations I hear in my classroom, as eager hands hold crumpled pieces of paper that survived the journey from school to home and back again. These dog-eared papers contain valuable pieces of data for the construction of a graph about houseplants. Even more valuable, these pages are the catalyst for a family engagement activity.

Asher shares his information and reports that he and his mom counted six houseplants in their home; he glues six clip-art images of houseplants to the graph. Liam tells us that he and his mom counted two; he glues down his pair of images. Dillon says that he and his dad counted sixty-six orchids in their orchid room. Wow! We're going to need a bigger graph. Furthermore, we've just learned that Dillon's dad has a passion for orchids. I now have another avenue to engage him—when I invite him to share orchids with us, he will gladly accept.

"A picture is worth a thousand words." A graph is a picture that young children can easily understand. Graphs are valuable tools that visually display relationships among data. They help us organize, analyze, and interpret information. Additionally, they appeal to young children, especially when the children provide the data.

Using a child's home as a data source is a wonderful way to engage both children and parents in a learning activity. Back in the classroom, students enjoy comparing and contrasting information as they discover and interpret similarities and differences, and practice graphing skills and mathematical reasoning.

I introduce this activity in a newsletter:

Houseplant Homework ... Well, maybe not homework, but we need your help!

Our new unit of study is our home habitat. When we study a habitat, we look at the living and non-living parts of the environment. We began with our non-living rocks. Now let's count living things — houseplants!

Please help your child count the number of houseplants inside your home (don't include outdoor plants).

Please fill out or have your child fill out the note below, and return it to class.

My name is_____.

I have _____ houseplants IN my home.

Below are instructions for the construction of the graph and questions to connect children with the information. It is important to have the graph constructed prior to the arrival of the children's data.

Constructing a picture graph:

- Label the child's name along the Y (left) axis of the graph.
- Number 1 to 20 across the X (top) axis of the graph.
- As an example, Brinnly has two houseplants. He finds his name and then places a small picture of a houseplant in each of two cells of the graph, moving horizontally from left to right.
- Brinnly glues his pictures to the graph.
- Ask open-ended questions about the graph: What do you notice about the number of houseplants? How did you know that? How will you know who has the most, least, or same amount of houseplants in their home?

Graph of the number of houseplants found in children's homes

What Are the Benefits of Involving Parents as Sources of Data?

Data can be gathered from any number of places, but choosing the child's home and family as resources lets parents know that they are valued and their involvement and contributions make a difference. Children also observe their parents as resources for information who can also assist with school skills.

I use this activity as a way to give parents an awareness of the Montessori early childhood math curriculum, in which counting objects matches one object to a quantity, creating a one-to-one correspondence. Once this is understood, I can explain the difference between the concrete object (the houseplant in this example) and the abstract math symbol that may be a 2 or a 66!

Once again, my newsletter serves as my method to communicate this activity with parents. In addition to the classroom information that is contained in my newsletters, my families come to anticipate activities to complete with their children. Sometimes, even families who usually overlook the weekly newsletter will participate—I've had handwritten notes come back to me with data reported. I can only assume it was prompted by a child eager to be included in the graph!

Variations on this Activity

When choosing sources for graphing data, I try to consider items that are fairly common in most homes, but are items that will create enough contrast to make the graph visually engaging. Some sources of data gathered from home could include:

- the number of people living in the house
- the number of pets
- the number of mirrors
- the number of windows
- the number of bicycles
- the number of spoons in the silverware drawer, etc.

Researching with Children: Involving Parents in Curriculum Themes

The bell rings on a Monday morning in the spring. Before the backpacks are hung on their hooks, skilled Australia researchers greet me with a wealth of new information.

- "Mrs. Harman! Koalas have two thumbs!"
- "Mrs. Harman! A baby kangaroo is the size of a jellybean!"
- "Mrs. Harman! Ayers Rock is the largest rock in the world!"

Then the unburdening of the backpacks begins, and the tattered pieces of paper emerge. They are encrypted with the children's unique early childhood spelling, and there is something quite special about this work. Along with the phonetic spelling and children's uneven handwriting, I see some well-developed, mature sentences and writing in an adult hand. Crikey! We're all learning about Australia together, mate!

Learning together, as children, parents, and teachers expand their relationship and partnership—that's what this book is all about! Inviting parents to become active participants in the process of researching and confirming the data can foster this relationship, while still keeping it doable for busy parents (the devices that we carry in our pockets and purses make the process of acquiring information fast and easy). There are plenty of resources available for continent studies about Australia. There is a wealth of material to develop units of study about the exotic biodiversity from the continent "Down Under."

The emphasis of this book, however, is not about developing interesting units of study; it is about engaging parents as educational partners and extending learning beyond the classroom environment. It is about empowering teachers, parents, and children to create dynamic relationships where all work together for the emotional and intellectual good of the child.

Here's an example of the research sheet that goes home with children:

Name:_____

I am learning about:_____

What I know:_____

What I want to know:_____

What I learned:_____

Research sheet

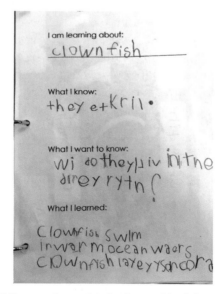

I am learning about:
clown fish

What I know:
they et kril.

What I want to know:
wi do theyl iv in tne
diney rytn (

What I learned:
Clowfish swim
in worm ocean waers
clownfish laye yys n cor

Child's research completed at home with adult support

Once parents have been introduced to the process of researching facts, they may find a much-needed strategy for responding to some of those big questions for which young children are infamous, like "Why is the sky blue?" and "Where do babies come from?" They can simply use the same format as the research sheet.

Here's another example:

> **Name:** *Lilly*
>
> **I am learning about:** *Babies*
>
> **What I know:** *Babies grow in their mommy's tummies.*

> (Next, get clarification on the specific question. Ask, "What do you want to know?" This is the important part that can prevent adults from oversharing.)

> **What I want to know:** *Are babies born through the mommy's belly button?*

> (Then, child and adult find the information together.)

> **What I learned:** *No, babies are born through a birth canal.*

Wow! That's pretty simple. The child received correct information from an adult, and the sweaty palm, red-faced encounter that most adults fear was avoided. This is an example of those questions I call "zingers," but this format can be applied to many questions from children.

Here's the invitation I send to parents (again, through my newsletter) to invite them to become "researchers."

Our Final Unit of Study

We will begin our final continent study for this school year: Australia and Australia's Great Barrier Reef!

Our field trips, visitors, and classroom works will all reflect this exciting continent! Our friends are invited to research and share "interesting facts" about Australia during morning circle time. For example, you and your child may have a picture of a kangaroo or a koala to share.

Research together, complete the attached form, and return it to school.

We'll be happy to share it and learn from one another!

PARENTS: Attached you will find our format for research. One-sentence research is sufficient, so this need not be a lengthy or time-consuming process. You may be amazed at the things you'll learn! We are, every day!

What Are the Benefits of Involving Parents in Researching with Children?

The National Association for the Education of Young Children publication *Informational Books in Early Childhood* reports on a study done by Pellegrini et al.

> Mothers asked more questions and introduced more vocabulary when reading aloud informational rather than narrative texts. (Duke, 2003)

This benefit is a worthy one; however, I see the social interaction that occurs between the child, the parent, and the teacher as equally important.

The teacher shares the simple method of research with child and parent and guides the topic based upon classroom theme; next, the child and the parent interact while gathering information; finally, the teacher reads the material back to the child and to the class as a whole. Parent, child, teacher, and classmates have a shared experience.

Noted relationship researcher J. M. Gottman (2001) suggests that shared experiences are a method to build relationships. Researching a common theme can be a vehicle for a shared experience, even though all the individuals involved may not interact face to face. In our classroom, everyone's presence and investment is evident upon the face of the child when their "research" is read to the group. Likewise, the group of children to whom the research is being read are benefitting from the efforts of all involved in the relationship and the information gathered.

Variations on this Activity

The possibilities for research topics are limitless, but you may want to begin with the themes you have already developed in your classrooms: apples, seasons, weather, holidays, transportation, colors, shapes, families, friends, community helpers, five senses, planets, plants, animals, dinosaurs (oh, the popularity of the animals and dinosaurs!), rocks, etc.

For example:

- I am learning about: *Apples.*
- What I know: *Apples are tasty.*
- What I want to know: *Why are apples good?*
- What I learned: *Apples have a special sugar called fructose.*

At-Home Volunteerism:
Laundry, Coordinating Field Trips, Preparing Art Materials
—You Name It!

- "I'd really like to volunteer in the classroom, but I have two jobs, and it's just not possible for me to take the time off."
- "I have young children at home and I don't think you'd want a toddler in your classroom."
- "If there's anything I can help with from home, I'd love to."
- "I feel so bad that I can't help at school like some of the other parents do."
- "Thanks for including me; we had fun working on this together."
- "I'm doing laundry this weekend anyway; just send it home with Tina."

I hear sentiments like this every week from parents who aren't able to be in the classroom but who nonetheless want to contribute. And I'm happy to have them!

In my experience, parents want to build relationships with their children's teachers—they have an innate desire to know the person or people who are caring for their children. Face-to-face interactions, however, can be rare because of work or family obligations. At-home volunteerism is a confetti activity that is less about the specifics of the activity and more about the child's observation of and role in the activity. By offering the volunteer opportunity and by performing it, the teacher and parent, respectively, are committing to one another for the benefit of the child.

The child's role is to transport materials to and from school. It could be a child taking home a bag of classroom laundry to wash together (what a great practical life experience!); a stack of "under construction" nametags for an upcoming field trip for a child and parent to fill out with students' names; or, perhaps, a new material for the classroom for the child and parent to assemble or complete.

Before sending home materials, I find it most helpful to have a sample prepared, if at all possible, to ensure success of the at-home project. I always include a note with written directions and a due date.

> Thank you for your willingness to volunteer at home! We will need these materials by _____.
>
> Please:
> - cut out the individual pictures
> - glue pictures to the upper left corner of the nametag
> - see sample included
>
> Thank you again for your valuable commitment and contribution!

What Are the Benefits of Involving Parents in At-Home Volunteerism?

Volunteerism in any setting creates the opportunity for a wealth of benefits: a sense of making a difference for others, fellowship in a community, learning new skills, and personal fulfillment, just to name a few. Volunteering for a child's classroom, whether physically or from home, also benefits children directly. Seeing their parents and teachers collaborating in this way shows children they matter, their learning matters, and the people surrounding them are working together for their benefit.

Finally, for parents who may not have fond memories of their own years at school, these activities offer a glimpse of what school can be—child-centered, joyful, and exciting. Whether you implement several of the activities in this chapter, just a few, or come up with your own, it is worth the effort to integrate a practice of engagement for parents, children, and teachers. Keep tossing the confetti—some will stick!

Chapter V
Classroom Volunteerism:
Ongoing Opportunities for Parents

Susan's mother has arrived to volunteer in her daughter's classroom. This energetic setting is much different from her quiet cubicle, where she, an introvert, feels more comfortable. She waits by the classroom door, shifting from foot to foot. The expression on her face is somewhere between discomfort and total fear. Fortunately, Susan looks up, runs to her mother's side, and leads her to the teacher.

"Oh dear," the teacher remarks, "It's been such a busy day, and I forgot you were coming. Let me see what I can find for you to do."

Susan's mother fidgets awkwardly, and the teacher rushes off nervously to find a task for her.

Susan is overjoyed to have her mother in the classroom! The adults, however, are less than thrilled.

Extra adult hands in the classroom … what teacher and learning environment wouldn't benefit from the assistance? *An unprepared one!* I'd like to tell you I've always had classroom volunteerism down to a science, but, in fact, that mortified teacher in the story above was me. And it could be me again, if it weren't for my co-teachers and some volunteer systems put in place. Classroom volunteers can be enormously helpful, but a great deal of organization and communication—both before the volunteers' arrival, and during their visits—is required to maximize their benefit.

First, decide which activities or areas of the classroom you wish to make available for volunteers. Of course, when designing opportunities for classroom volunteerism, it is important to consult school policies regarding volunteerism and confidentiality. Some schools have strict policies that prohibit delivery of curriculum by anyone other than the teacher. In that case, enrichment activities are the most appropriate use of classroom volunteers. In this chapter, I list volunteer activities that work well in many early childhood and lower elementary settings.

Next, determine a method for organizing the individuals who will be volunteering. You can ask a classroom parent to be the volunteer coordinator; that person can schedule volunteers and inform them of their tasks. Or there are many free online resources that can organize volunteers: SignUpGenius, VolunteerSpot, YourVolunteers, or iVolunteer are just a few. You can use them to describe volunteer activities and list open slots so parents can sign up. Even if you use an online organizer, it's still helpful to print out (or have your parent volunteer coordinator print out) a list of monthly volunteers or weekly volunteer activities, so you're never in the awkward position of trying to find something for a parent to do.

Cooking

Cooking activities at school can be great fun for parent volunteers and children alike. Parents often have special family recipes they like to share, and children always enjoy the cooking process. Additionally, some children also enjoy tasting school-made dishes, and occasionally, some even try something new!

Advance planning is the key; the type of dish you can make will depend on the cooking facilities available in your classroom or at your school. Ingredients will need to be purchased prior to the experience. Good planning can help to set clear expectations, which in turn lead to positive experiences for the volunteers, the teacher, and the children.

See Chapter IV, *Extending Classroom Experiences*, page 38 for ideas about cooking at home.

Guiding questions for organizing cooking experiences:

- What general information should be explained to the volunteer?
- What is the date and time of the experience? About how long will it take?
- Who chooses the recipe?
- Do any students have food allergies?
- Does school policy forbid any specific ingredients?
- Who purchases and provides funding for the ingredients?
- Who is responsible for gathering cooking utensils?
- Where will the cooking experience occur?
- How many children will participate? How will those children be chosen?
- When, where, and how is the finished dish shared with classmates?
- Who is responsible for cleanup of the cooking area and return of utensils?

Sewing

Sewing and textile work provides children with practice of practical life skills which enhance fine motor skills and refine hand-eye coordination. Textiles such as yarn and fabric offer children opportunities to manipulate various textures and colors, concepts familiar to Montessori children who have explored the Sensorial materials.

As I mentioned in Chapter III, *Personal Touches*, page 29, I have been blessed with a delightful and generous parent volunteer. Mrs. Reddipalli is going on her seventh year of sewing with the children in my class, even though her daughter is now in fifth grade. Together, she and I have implemented a variety of experiences for the children: sewing running stitches, button sewing, cross stitching, sewn book bindings, yarn doll construction, mobile making, sock puppets, weaving, and quilting. Sewing activities are easiest for parent volunteers to implement when the lesson is well planned (all materials, including directions, are gathered and prepared), and there is a sample of the finished product to use as a template.

Guiding questions for organizing sewing experiences:

- What general information should be explained to the volunteer?
- What is the date and time of the experience? About how long will it take?
- Is there a sample of the project?
- Who is purchasing or gathering the necessary materials?
- Is all equipment (sewing machine, etc.) in the classroom? If not, who will provide it? Is it in working order?
- How is each child's project identified? Will names go on the front or back of the project? Is there a nametag placed on the project?
- How many children may participate at one time?
- What is to be done with completed projects?
- Who is responsible for the cleanup of the project?

Gardening

Gardening experiences can be large-scale (a community garden) or small-scale (sprouting individual plants in tiny cups of soil). Horticultural activities provide children with the opportunity to observe the life cycle of a living thing. Germinating lima bean seeds in a plastic bag with a damp paper towel and a sunny window will demonstrate the development of roots and the sprouting of the stem and leaves. Plants that sprout quickly inspire awe in young children and demonstrate the need for humans to care for the plant's delicate natural environment—the little plant's well-being is in the hands of the child responsible for the moisture of the paper towel. Regardless of the size or scope of the gardening project, planning, communication, and organization are essential for a positive outcome.

Guiding questions for organizing gardening experiences:

- What general information should be explained to the volunteer?
- What is the date and time of the experience? About how long will it take?
- Is the project outdoors or indoors? If outdoors, will a staff member need to accompany the volunteer?
- Is it a planting project or something else (weeding, etc.)?
- Will the project require follow-up maintenance (weeding, watering, harvesting)?
- If weeding, are there photos available to help identify weeds from valued plants?
- If watering, where are the water sources and water containers?
- If harvesting, where is the harvest to be stored? What is the policy for tasting? (Brightly-colored, ripe cherry tomatoes and strawberries are often hard to resist!)
- Are tools, gloves, or special clothing required?
- How many children may participate at one time?
- Who is responsible for the cleanup of the project?

Classroom Parties

Classroom parties can be wonderful social events for parents and children alike, and an ideal opportunity for parent volunteering. They require meticulous planning, since typically all children participate at the same time (and are especially energetic and excited on party days!). I find that classroom party planning is most successful when tasks are divided up among the volunteers.

For example, a planning committee can develop the activities: games, snacks, or crafts. Another group can be responsible for the implementation of those activities on the party day, while still another group can shepherd children from one activity to another; a final group can take charge of cleanup and putting the classroom back together again. Clear communication and limits will help make classroom parties enjoyable for everyone.

Guiding questions for organizing party experiences:

- What general information should be explained to the volunteer?
- What is the date and time of the experience?
- What are the responsibilities of the volunteer, and when will they be explained?
- Who is responsible for planning activities?
- Are there any themes that should be kept in mind (holiday, etc.)?
- What are the activities?
- Who is responsible for the materials?
- Who is responsible for implementing the plans for the activities?
- How are children organized or grouped for the activities?
- What indicates the party or activity is over?
- Who is responsible for the cleanup of the party?

Field Trips

The concrete experiences offered by field trips create sensory learning connections for early childhood students. No book, app, or video can replace the real experience (and the sights, sounds, smells, textures, and tastes) of a field trip. The options are numerous: apple farms, pumpkin patches, fire stations, and zoos are just a few of the locales that can offer a stimulating outing. Field trips are also a chance for parents to volunteer as chaperones, serving as extra sets of eyes and hands for teachers.

While having parent chaperones can be useful, it's important to keep in mind that the change in location, change in routine, and the excitement about the presence of family members can result in children exhibiting some behavior challenges. So, as always, planning in advance and communicating clearly is vital to maximize the effectiveness of the volunteers, so everyone can enjoy a day of adventures.

I have 31 children in my class, and two extremely helpful assistants. During field trips, we divide our class list into thirds, and my assistants and I are each responsible for one group of 10 or 11 children. (It is much quicker to count 10 or 11 excited, bouncing heads than 31!) Each group has a unique nametag, assembled in advance by an at-home parent volunteer.

For example, for a field trip to the pumpkin patch, we might have one nametag displaying pumpkin blossoms, another with green pumpkins, and a third with orange pumpkins. In addition to the group-specific artwork, the front of each nametag bears a child's name. The back of each nametag lists the school's name, phone number, and an emergency phone number (usually my cell phone). Each nametag is pinned on the child's clothing. Parent volunteers join the group to which their child is assigned.

I ask the parents to remain with their group but assume responsibility for only their child on the field trip. The parent volunteers are part of either my small group or the small group of one of my assistants. The parents are able to visit with their child and their child's friends and follow my lead in indicating points of interest to the children, while the responsibility of the safety of the group resides with the teaching staff. Overall, this arrangement is more pleasant for the parent and less stressful for me.

At the end of the field trip, one or more of the parent volunteers may choose to take their child with them instead of returning to school. In this case, I ask the parent to remove the child's nametag and return it to me. Then I pin the nametag to my clothing as a visible reminder that the child is no longer with the group.

Guiding questions for organizing field trip experiences:

- What general information should be explained to the volunteer?
- What specific responsibilities will the volunteer have?
- What is the date and time of the experience?
- Will volunteers be responsible for their own child, a group of children, or just provide general support?
- How will volunteers know the names of children?

- Will volunteers be required to remain with the teacher or may they leave the group?
- After the field trip, what is the procedure for a child to leave the field trip with a family member?

Special Talents

Parents can be untapped wells of expertise. Those talented adults may range from musicians to builders, tailors to martial artists, and gardeners to ping-pong champions! Many adults, however, may not realize that their own skills, knowledge, or interests can be adapted to provide a rich learning experience in the classroom (while at the same time building parent engagement and the parent-teacher relationship).

At open houses, parent-teacher conferences, or through newsletter surveys or casual conversations, invite parents to share their talents. I find that using curriculum themes as prompts works well. For example, during a rainforest unit, Dillon's dad visited our classroom twice—once to share some of his orchids, and another time to share the family's pet snakes!

Adults may need your guidance to ensure that they share their talent and expertise in a way that is accessible to young children. Something concrete for the children to see, hear, touch, smell, or taste will make the experience rich and meaningful. I had a grandparent bring in a completed duck decoy as well as a block of wood, a partially carved decoy, a rough carved decoy, and a smooth unfinished decoy. The children could touch all the decoys as he talked to them about ducks (he left out the hunting part for my young audience). Another parent gave a live demonstration of cake decorating. Photographs that illustrate an activity sequence—for example, images taken weekly as a house is being built to show its progress—are also helpful.

Discussing the structure of the presentation with a parent beforehand can also ensure things go smoothly. I've found 15–20 minutes to be an ideal length for a presentation that will hold the attention of young children. Curious children will always have questions, so allowing them to ask a limited number of questions enhances the experience.

Guiding questions for organizing special-talent experiences:

- What general information should be explained to the volunteer?
- What is the date and time of the experience?
- How long is the display of talent?
- How much space is needed?
- Are any materials needed? If so, who supplies the materials?
- Is this an experience for the whole class, a small group, or should it be presented to one child at a time?
- Will the display of talent experience require cleanup? If so, who is responsible?

Refinishing Projects

Thrift shops, garage sales, and even a neighbor's trash—these can be picking wonderlands for classroom refinishing projects in which parent volunteers engage. Near the hand-washing station in my classroom, a beautifully framed mirror delights my children each day as they admire their beautiful reflections. This mirror was once an unattractive, framed mirror that I found for $2 at a thrift shop. The original frame was covered with faux reptile patterned paper.

A series of classroom volunteers provided lessons on how to sand. They supervised the children as they sanded the frame to reveal a surface ready for a new façade, relieving the frame of its greenish faux scales. They oversaw the children as they taped the mirror with painter's tape to protect the glass. These volunteers who supervised the children during this semester-long project happened to be dads and uncles.

Refinished thrift store mirror

The music teacher who had been working with the children on musical notation provided us with some interesting discarded sheet music that the children ripped into strips. The volunteers helped to shape the pieces into manageable 2" x 1" pieces. Finally, the pieces of paper were secured by painting a decoupage medium onto the frame and placing the paper atop the glue. A dad volunteer added the finishing touch. After the children painted one final coat of glue over the entire surface of the frame and it dried, he removed the protective painter's tape from the mirror. Goodbye faux reptile skin and hello musical frame that is sung to regularly!

Refinishing a piece of furniture may require sanding (children love the protective masks and goggles), painting, reconditioning, or covering a surface. This process can take an extended period of time to complete—sometimes even an entire school year. As a result, these projects may require the efforts of multiple adults and children, all working together to restore an item. The projects provide an environmental lesson on repurposing, and the finished creation can be a lovely addition to the classroom. More importantly, it is an opportunity for a meaningful classroom volunteer experience.

Ideas for refinishing objects or furnishings can be found on DIY websites such as doityourself.com, pinterest.com, and handsonaswegrow.com. I am often on the lookout for interesting items that lend themselves for refinishing and upcycling projects when I visit thrift and antique shops. Typically, I plan the project with a sequence of steps to be implemented by several volunteers. When I don't have a parent volunteer to supervise the project, the project is stored and unavailable until the next volunteer arrives to help. Dads, uncles, and grandpas love to volunteer for these refinishing projects, but of course I welcome any qualified and interested volunteer.

Guiding questions for organizing refinishing experiences:

- What general information should be explained to the volunteer?
- What is the date and time of the experience?
- Is the project expected to be completed in one session or is it an ongoing opportunity?
- What space is needed?

- Are any materials needed? If so, who supplies the materials?
- Is this an experience for the whole class, a small group, or an individual?
- Who is responsible for cleanup?

Efforts to Engage Male Volunteers

It is true that most classroom volunteers are women, and it is also true that children need both male and female role models. Often deliberate efforts are necessary to recruit men for volunteer activities. As with any volunteers, find out what special talents and interests they have. Perhaps a dad or granddad loves gardening, woodworking, music, or cooking and can make a special presentation to the class. Over the years, male volunteers have been involved in many projects in my class.

My school has made a conscious effort to recruit male volunteers. Often the volunteer is a student's father, but once or twice a year stepdads, grandfathers, uncles, adult siblings, and other significant males spend an entire day at school. They perform duties including, but not limited to, helping with traffic control at drop-off and pick-up times, walking the perimeter of the building to make certain the doors are locked, augmenting school security, assisting the custodial staff, and helping out in classrooms.

This program is so popular that there is often a waiting list managed by one of our school office staff who plans each hour of the volunteer's day with specific locations, times, and tasks. In addition, two hours of the day are dedicated to being in their child's classroom. The volunteer and their child have lunch together.

As usual, be sure the volunteers have a general idea of what they will be doing when in the classroom and be sure they understand that the behavioral expectations for children must be clear and consistent. (Roughhousing is a fun activity better served in another setting!)

There is no simple formula to creating inclusive communities. Efforts made to include all parents in volunteer activities demonstrate a shift toward greater inclusion. By welcoming fathers and other male family members and acknowledging their unique presence to children, we open one more avenue of inclusivity and create the opportunity for new conversations.

On the national level, the organization called WATCH D.O.G.S. (Dads of Great Students) strives to get more fathers and father-figures involved in their child's life at school. Check out their website for programs available.

Sanding woodblocks with a WATCH D.O.G.S. volunteer

Guiding questions for organizing male volunteer experiences:

- What is the date and time of the experience?
- How do male volunteers schedule their opportunity?
- What activity is expected of the volunteer?
- Who creates the schedule?
- How are teachers notified of the volunteer's schedule?
- How will the program be implemented in the school setting?

Chapter VI
Classroom Volunteerism:
Academic Support

Mrs. Williams confidently enters my classroom on a busy Tuesday morning. The children, including her son Miles, are already engaged in their morning work and a pleasant hum of children's voices and activity fill the environment. Mrs. Williams walks past a group of children who are working on a small group literacy lesson. She quietly says hello to me with respect to not disrupt the children's concentration, gives Miles a hug on her way through the classroom, and walks directly to the shelf where the classroom volunteer folders are kept. She opens the folder, finds the names of several children, scans the room for a child who is between activities and walks over to one of those children and says, "Would you like to read with me?"

What? A parent enters a classroom and the hum of activity doesn't deteriorate to a disruptive cacophony? It doesn't have to. Actually, it can be a rewarding activity for parents and children alike. The parent has an opportunity to support the learning of their child and other children gain greater understanding of child development through observation. Witnessing the learning environment they have chosen for their child, parents often leave a little starry-eyed as they contemplate the many abilities of young children in an environment prepared just for them. The smooth integration of a parent into an early childhood academic environment, however, requires deliberate attention to detail, organization, and brief training at the onset.

I call this type of work "academic support volunteering." In my classroom, I have found that sharing a glimpse of the Montessori method can be a bonding experience for teachers and volunteers. Montessori education is a method that is deeply entrenched in philosophy, pedagogy, and rigorous training. For parents who volunteer in an academic support role, the opportunity demystifies some of the method and demonstrates the learning that occurs through use of the three-period lesson and Montessori materials. Parts of the Montessori math curriculum seem especially well suited to this purpose.

An essential part of Montessori education, as well as any effective early childhood program, is the provision of multiple opportunities for practice towards mastery. Some children require a lot of repetition, adult support and attention, as well as multiple successes, to acquire mastery. Parent volunteers are capable of re-presenting an activity for reinforcement, which allows children to repeat an activity as needed.

Schools and teachers have varying levels of comfort when allowing volunteers to supplement instruction. In some settings, it may be contrary to school policy or teaching philosophy to include parent volunteers in this role. If engaging parent volunteers for academic support makes you feel uncomfortable, perhaps include your classroom parent volunteers in a different role. Teachers who enlist parent volunteers to complement instruction must remember that initial lessons should be demonstrated to the child by the teacher, since even the most capable volunteer cannot supplant the experience and knowledge of a professional educator.

Engaging parents as academic support volunteers creates a powerful parent-teacher connection. Because of work commitments, many parents won't have the opportunity to be a part of their child's educational setting, but the parent who does can take the methods learned in the classroom back to their home and community. They will be better able to explain and advocate for the educational method they chose for their child. And on a couple of occasions, parents have been so enamored with the classroom that they chose to pursue a career in education. Additionally, engaging parents in the role of academic support creates intentional one-on-one or small group connections that many children desire and some require.

What about the deliberate attention to detail, organization, and brief training at the onset that makes this form of engagement possible? First, timing is essential. I ask even the most eager volunteers to wait 6-8 weeks from the beginning of the school year before entering the classroom or joining us for lunch. Children need to be well settled into their classroom routine, able to separate from parents easily at drop-off, and navigate the classroom with independence and confidence. Children who are not yet autonomous may find it difficult to say goodbye at the end of the parent's session and may cling to their parent instead of pursuing their own work.

Secondly, I believe it necessary to share and train parents on some basics of adult classroom behavior (remember: norms in the adult workplace are quite different than in the classroom). I explain that adults should demonstrate the same grace and courtesy we expect the children to follow (quiet voices when speaking, no interrupting of children who are working, and respectful care of materials) before we proceed to delivery of lessons. This part of the process of training parents will be worth the time investment.

Your parent volunteers will require direction regarding the "what" and "how" of a particular lesson. I find that the more specifics I can offer the volunteer about the lesson, the more helpful they can be. I always ask the volunteer to read through the lesson plan and then observe the lesson as I present it to a child. Most children are generally delighted by the presence of a parent in their classroom. They relish the opportunity to help any adult (often their own parent) by demonstrating the lesson and the work procedure. Once the adult volunteer understands the basics of the lesson, they can work with children who need additional practice.

I keep two volunteer folders, one for reading support and one for math support. Each folder contains specific lesson plans that include photographs of the materials. The folders always remain in the same location, so volunteers can easily find and return them. Additionally, I provide volunteers with a spreadsheet checklist with each child's name so they can note which children have received what kind of support. What follows are examples of lessons volunteers in my classroom have been able to support successfully.

Guiding questions for organizing academic support experiences:

- What general information should be explained to the volunteer (where to work in the classroom, how to invite a child to work, how long to expect a lesson to last, where to return materials)?

- Has confidentiality been discussed with the volunteer? Volunteers agree not to disclose information about any child's educational progress with anyone outside of the classroom. Some schools have a written agreement that volunteers sign regarding this matter.
- What is the date and time of the experience?
- What activity is going to be explained to the volunteer?
- Where can the materials be found?
- What is the procedure for volunteers to instruct children?
- Are materials present and complete for the volunteer?

Reading Volunteer

Introduction

Echo Reading is extremely effective for the youngest children in our class as the text is designed to be easily remembered through repetitive language. Knowledge of sounds or puzzle words is not a prerequisite.

Materials

- Container with multiple copies of short, leveled books with predictable language (also known as "guided readers")
- Echo Reading Procedure (in folder)
- Echo Reading Record Keeping Spreadsheet (in folder)

Echo Reading Procedure

1. Choose 2–3 children from the list to read with you. Children whose names are listed near one another are at similar levels of experience with reading. Begin reading with children who have read the fewest titles. All children have previously been introduced to the Echo Reading process.

2. Give a copy of the book to each child.

3. Discuss the cover and ask the children to predict what they think the story is about based upon the illustration. Accept all answers equally. Say, "Let's read to find out."

4. Read the text while pointing to each word. Read one page, then the children "echo" as a group by pointing with a finger and reading the text. Continue with the next page, then the children echo. Complete the book in this manner.

5. Invite the first child to read to the group. Everyone else is a "listener" and follows the text with their finger.

6. Do not correct the child if what they "read" is not quite right.

7. Invite the next child to read while others are listeners.

8. Continue until all the children have had a chance to be the "reader."

9. Finish by comparing the story to the predictions.

10. Record the date the child read the title on the Echo Reading Record Keeping Spreadsheet.

Echo Reading Record Keeping Spreadsheet

Children's Names	Book Title A	Book Title B	Book Title C	
Nadja	9/15	10/4		
Bobby	9/21	10/4	11/1	
Guillermo	9/15	11/1		

Math Volunteer

Instructions for the Teacher

Be sure the Math folder for volunteers contains the following:

- Photograph of Math material located on the Math shelf
- Math Support Procedures
- Math Record Keeping Spreadsheet with names of children who would benefit from replication of a previous lesson demonstrated by the classroom teacher

Activity I: Montessori Sandpaper Numerals

Material

- Green Sandpaper Numeral Cards

Procedure

1. Invite a child from the list to work with the material: "May I work with the Sandpaper Numerals with you?" Ask the child to put out a work rug.
2. Remove all the cards from the box and place them face up on the rug in random order.

3. Ask the child to name the numerals in random order.

4. Slide any unknown numerals to the bottom of the rug, saying "This is a good one to practice."

5. Place numerals already known back into box.

6. Ask the child to choose one numeral card from the bottom of the rug.

7. Trace the sandpaper numeral on the card, using index and middle finger, and say its name. Ask the child to trace the numeral, and say its name. Repeat for the second numeral.

8. Point to the first numeral, say its name (6) and ask the child to repeat. Repeat for the second numeral (9).

9. Ask the child to find the numeral 9. Ask the child to find the numeral 6.

10. Mix up the cards and repeat step 7 until you think the child knows the names of the numerals.

11. End the lesson by mixing the cards one last time. Point to one of the numerals and ask, "What is this?"

Activity II: Teen Memory Game

Material

- A Mortensen math material in a pouch

Procedure

1. Invite a child from the list to work with the material: "May I work with the Teen Memory Game with you?" Ask the child to put out a work rug.

2. Remove the contents of the pouch. Place the number cards face down in a pile. Lay out the number rods from 1 to 10 creating a step.

3. Remove the first card from the pile. Look at it. Do not show the child the card. Slide it face down partially under the rug with a tip sticking out from the rug.

4. Remove the 10 rod and the appropriate unit rod and place them side-by-side. For example, if the card reads 14, place the 10 rod and the 4 rod side-by-side.

5. Ask the child to count the total number of squares on the rods to determine that your number is 14.

6. Show the child the card, place it above the rods, and say, "The one tells us one ten bar and the four tells us four units." Point to the rods and say 14.

7. Return the card to the pouch. Return the rods to the step.

8. Then ask the child to take a card from the pile, look at the card, place rods on the rug for you to count, and slide the card face down under the rug as you had done. Point to and count each square on the rods and make your "guess" for their number.

9. Ask the child to remove the card from under the rug and place it above the rods. If the card does not match the rods as described in step 6, help the child find the correct rods.

10. The child returns the rods to the step and returns the number card to the pouch.

11. Continue the game alternating child and adult turns until each card is used and returned to the pouch.

Activity III: Ten Boards — Sequential Counting

Material

- Montessori Ten Boards

Procedure

1. Invite a child from the list to work with the materials. "May I work with the Ten Boards with you?" Begin with a child who has the fewest tallies. Ask the child to put out a work rug.

2. Remove the two boards from the box. Lay them out vertically, one below the other, on the rug. Place the cards in order in a pile with the 1 card on top. Ask the child to read (or sing) the numbers on the ten boards while you point (10, 20, 30, 40, 50, 60, 70, 80, 90).

3. Point to the first number and ask the child to name it. Take the 1 card from the pile and slide it into place over the 0, turning 10 into 11. Ask child to read "11." If necessary tell the child, "This is 11." Remove the 1 card and place it face down on the rug.

4. Slide the 2 card over the 0 of the 10. Ask the child to read "12." If necessary tell the child, "This is 12." Remove the 2 card and place it face down on top of the 1 card.

5. Place the 3 card over the 0. The child reads "13." Remove the 3 card and place it face down on top of the 2 card.

6. Continue until 19.

7. Point to 20 and ask child to name it. Count (or sing) by 10s if the child does not recognize 20. Turn the cards over so the 1 card is on top.

8. Slide the 1 card over the 0 of the 20 and ask the child to read "21." Remove the card and place it face down on the rug.

9. Continue placing cards over the zero until reaching 29. Repeat this procedure for 30, 40, 50, etc.

Math Record Keeping Spreadsheet

- Begin with a child who has the fewest tallies.
- Follow Math Procedure for the specific lesson indicated.
- Make a tally each time a child receives support. Some children will need a lot of repetition.

Sandpaper Numerals		Teens		Ten Board Sequential Counting	
	Jackson		Colin		Carol
III		II		I	
	Bobby		Sebastian		Ryan
II		IIII		HHH	
	Alice		LaShawne		Kanisha
HHH II		II			

Chapter VII
Sharing Successes:
Celebrating Accomplishments Together

"Whenever I ask Clara what she did at school, the answer is always the same: 'Nothing!' If I press her, she might say she had lunch, played outside, and maybe had snack. I have no idea what goes on behind those school doors. What does she do all day?"

Does this story sound familiar? A Montessori teacher's answer could be, "She constructed her learning through refined sensory experiences and the manipulation of didactic, concrete materials that led to the development of practical life skills, numeracy, literacy, and greater understanding of her connections with the world around her."

Or, perhaps, "She prepared her own snack, sequenced cubes from largest to smallest, manipulated spindles toward greater understanding of quantity, traced sandpaper letters, and explored a puzzle map of the continents."

Both answers, while accurate, are loaded with a tremendous amount of educational jargon and will probably not satisfy Clara's mother. Rightfully so! Professional terminology is often confusing to those outside the profession. I think of dinnertime conversations with my computer programmer husband, Chris. I'm often left wondering if I have heard how to retrieve a lost file or sequence the launch of the space shuttle!

The experience may be the same for parents of young children in Montessori and other early learning settings. Child development, methods of instruction, and sensitive periods or windows of optimal learning are valuable conversations between educational professionals, but to the outsider, including parents, these topics may increase a divide between families and teacher.

Furthermore, if an adult (the teacher) speaks for the child (Clara), it strips her of the opportunity to respond and demonstrate her understanding of the work she has completed. We wouldn't want Clara to miss the opportunity to communicate the joy she experienced when mastering an activity, or the courage she displayed when trying a new material to expand her learning.

Realistically, teachers do not have the time for detailed daily conferences with parents about the activity of their young child. So, what can we do to preserve Clara's opportunity to share with her mother, honor Clara's mother's request, and make communication manageable for the teacher? The answer lies within Clara. Tools to aid her to recall her day respect each party's needs. Also, chances are Clara's lovely description of her day in her own words or pictures will be much less complex and more charming than the space shuttle dinner conversation that still puzzles me!

Maria Montessori wrote:

> A child who has become master of his acts through long and repeated exercises, and who has been encouraged by the pleasant and interesting activities in which he has been engaged, is a child filled with health and joy and [is] remarkable for his calmness and discipline. (1990, p. 92)

"Ask Me About ..." Stickers

One solution to Clara's "nothing" answer may be "Ask Me About ..." stickers. I print the words "Ask me about ..." on 1" x 2⅝" laser labels, leaving some blank space underneath. Then, as children complete work throughout the day, my assistant or I can write some details about the activity on the sticker. For example, Clara's sticker could read, "Ask me about ... the sounds 'm' and 'a'." The sticker can go on a piece of paper or on Clara's shirt at dismissal.

When Clara's mother sees it, she will have a starting point for a conversation with her daughter. Asking a specific question, guided by the "Ask me about ..." sticker, may elicit a more complete answer from Clara. This will help her mother learn more about Clara's work at school, and it also can serve as an occasion for Clara to demonstrate understanding of a lesson she received and show pride in her accomplishment.

Student Self-Reporting

Young children are delightfully honest! I always know that when I go to school with a blemish or any other visible flaw, I'll likely have it helpfully pointed out by a student. I've learned to laugh and embrace these moments. I try to guide that innate honesty toward helping children develop self-assessment, evaluation, and reflection skills (as well as the best ways to communicate information to others).

Metacognition (understanding one's own thinking) helps children reflect on their feelings and behaviors, and develops the traits of accountability, responsibility, and courage. I like to use a "Workday Report" to help build metacognition in my students. It also does double duty by communicating information about the school day to parents, decreasing the chance that a parent will get the dreaded "nothing" response.

A workday report can be utilized in different ways. I've used it most frequently as a tool when I am consciously observing a particular child in my classroom. I prepare a stack of workday reports with the children's names already on the forms. Each day I complete the form with a child at the end of the day as we reflect on the day's activities together. I find having one child chosen before the day begins helps create a snapshot of a typical school day, reflects the child's usual activities, and makes the task of completing the report manageable for me.

Younger children will need more support in completing the report. Typically, they dictate their favorite and most challenging work while I write. We discuss a "goal" for the following day's work choice that I record on the form. Then the child can independently circle the "fireworks" section of the form to reflect on their work habits for the day. The honesty of children never ceases to amaze me, as they will often reflect on their work habits with astute accuracy.

Kindergarteners often begin by drawing pictures to complete their workday report. Eventually, words and sentences appear. Older children can exercise their writing skills while they complete the workday report independently. Of course, their writing is peppered with invented spelling. This adds to the charm that entices parents to read the report and ask their child questions for clarification.

Occasionally children will ask to complete a report without my prompting. This occurs most frequently when children have observed one another using the tool. Modeling becomes a very powerful motivator as the younger children want to be like the "big kids" and have paperwork to take home.

Child displays self-reporting Workday Report

Another motivator can be the child's pride in their work and their desire to share it with a grown-up at home. One day Brian, who was 5 and has challenges with completing tasks, was particularly proud of the three activities he completed throughout the course of his day. He asked to complete a report just so he could show it to his mom!

Work Plans

In some settings, children, especially kindergarten-age children, keep track of their daily work on a work plan. My daily work plan format can be found in Chapter II, *Getting to Know Each Other*, p. 19. I have also been fortunate to observe in several settings where children record their daily accomplishments and can later recount their work to their parents.

Most work plans organize the work by the areas of the classroom. Some are open-ended allowing children to choose their activities, some require a teacher to assist in recording or verifying work, and some are shared with parents on a daily or weekly basis.

My work plan also provides children with a location to record their "random acts of kindness," which many parents report to be of significant importance. Children record, or someone records for them, the occasions when they have cared for themselves, others, or their environments.

Regardless of the format, a work plan can be an effective tool for communicating accomplishments to parents.

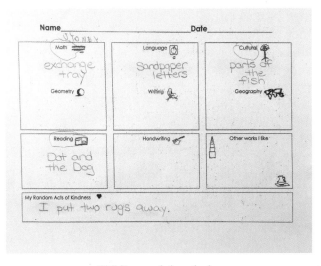

Child's recorded work plan

Chapter VIII
Special Occasions and Celebrations:
Social Opportunities to Deepen the
Parent-Teacher-Child Relationship

I Wandered Lonely as a Cloud

by William Wordsworth

I wandered lonely as a cloud
That floats on high o'er vales and hills,
When all at once I saw a crowd,
A host, of golden daffodils;
Beside the lake, beneath the trees,
Fluttering and dancing in the breeze.

Continuous as the stars that shine
And twinkle on the Milky Way,
They stretched in never-ending line
Along the margin of a bay:
Ten thousand saw I at a glance,
Tossing their heads in sprightly dance.

The waves beside them danced; but they
Out-did the sparkling waves in glee:
A poet could not but be gay,
In such a jocund company:
I gazed—and gazed—but little thought
What wealth the show to me had brought:

For oft, when on my couch I lie
In vacant or in pensive mood,
They flash upon that inward eye
Which is the bliss of solitude;
And then my heart with pleasure fills,
And dances with the daffodils.

"Today, McAlister told me that if he could build a time machine, he would go back to the day that he first entered your classroom. If that doesn't speak volumes!"
— McAlister's mom

It seems McAlister (as well as Wordsworth) was in a reflective mood! Wordsworth's poem was inspired by an outing with his sister, Dorothy, in 1802. It begins with loneliness and ends with his heart in the company of (and in relationship with) flowers, the sea, and stars. Later, the mere remembrance of the encounter causes his heart to dance. I interpret the memory of the daffodils as an allegory for a personal relationship. Though I am by no means a poetry expert, I do know that the thought of a close relationship can cause one's heart to fill with pleasure.

Being with others feels good and causes our brain to release what Dr. Loretta Graziano Breuning (2012) calls "happy chemicals"—dopamine, serotonin, oxytocin, and endorphins. Engaging in social activities that deepen our personal relationships washes our brains with feelings of well-being, and our hearts "with pleasure fill." I return to this idea often as I think about engaging with parents.

Enriching the Affective Domain of Your Students

My career in education has blessed me with multiple teaching settings (in five states and on two continents, in private and public schools, and in traditional and Montessori environments) in which to develop and enrich children's intellectual skills. I am also concerned with children's growth in what Dr. Benjamin Bloom called the affective domain—the area that includes emotions, attitudes, motivations, feelings, values, and relationships.

Through integrating special occasions and celebrations in the classroom, I wish to enrich the affective domain and trigger the release of "happy chemicals" in the brain. Affective domain skills progress from simply receiving ideas to displaying consistent value-based behavior. It is my sincerest wish to entice teachers, children, and parents to value one another, recognize the vast potential inherent within each of us, and find joy in doing so.

I'm sure your school has established a wealth of celebrations that take many social forms. The potential for celebration is limited only by your imagination. I ask you to think of how you might add to your existing events, or integrate new ones, with the intention of deepening parent engagement. What follows are a few of the yearly events at my school that make my heart dance, as with the daffodils.

Take-Your-Parent-to-School Day

My son Anthony loved Take-Your-Child-to-Work day. He would meet his dad's co-workers, go to lunch, and, most importantly, enjoy spending the day with someone special. A Take-Your-Parent-to-School day is a similar social event. It is an opportunity for parent, child, and teacher to strengthen their relationship, and, of equal importance, this event is an opportunity for children to share their friends, their classroom, and their independent work with someone special. The children guide their guests through the work they have selected to share while I act as observer and resource only if questions arise.

Winter Holiday Celebrations

What better way to develop partnership with families than by inviting them to a day in their child's life? Each year, I invite parents to a classroom "Winter Celebration." I plan the event around the winter holidays, when festive gatherings are common and employers may be more likely to allow time-off. I keep the event short (less than an hour and a half) for parents who need to get back to work. To give parents ample notice and increase the likelihood of participation, I plan in advance. I first publish the date and time of the event in an October newsletter, and then I give weekly reminders.

Because of the size of my classroom, I divide the class into two groups, staggering the celebration times. Having two celebrations on two separate days is another possibility.

Please join us for our Winter Celebration!

On Tuesday, December 13, we will host our winter celebration. We will share a song, our work, and our "school-made" snacks.

Due to limited space in our classroom, each child may invite only one adult to attend.

Younger friends'(preschoolers) guests may attend from 8:30 – 9:35. Older friends' (kindergarteners) guests may attend from 9:55 – 11:00.

Adults who are not invited to this celebration may attend our Spring Fling later this year.

- -

Please RSVP so we may notify the office of your attendance and plan for our guests.

_____ (adult's name) will attend the Winter Celebration on December 13 as

_____'s (child's name) guest.

This event is a rare instance when I urge families to commit to attending; that way each child has someone special to host. If parents are unavailable, I work with them to brainstorm another possible family member or friend who can step in. As a last resort, a sibling or school staff member can serve as the child's guest. Notice that I use the singular word "guest" in the invitation.

This event is an opportunity for children to share the work they do regularly in the classroom. I limit each child to one adult guest because children need space in the classroom to demonstrate their work. 15 or 16 additional adults in my classroom takes up a great deal of room that ordinarily would be space where children complete their work. Since this is not a social event, but an occasion for parents to observe the child's daily activity, space must be preserved to allow for their work.

Often new families are concerned about their child having to choose only one family member or friend to attend this event. Their concerns are quieted with disclosure of a similar end-of-the-year event that I call the "Spring Fling." This is my end of the year social class picnic where children of two parent families can invite the parent who did not attend the Winter Celebration. Actually, the more guests the merrier and if the spring weather cooperates in Nebraska, where I live, both parents may attend!

My events have several components:

- a group song or other group activity that serves as a great photo op for parents;
- a shared snack usually prepared as a cooking activity prior to the event (with a cooking volunteer as discussed in Chapter IV, *Extending Classroom Experiences*, p. 38), which is served by the children to their guest;
- and most importantly, a list of specific activities the child has chosen to share with their guest. The work list helps children remain focused upon the activities they have chosen, and helps the guest remain engaged with the child (rather than spending time chatting with other adults). Remember, parents may have a vastly different occupation other than working with children and clear directions for adults to observe while the child demonstrates and explains the work will help them to be successful in your classroom.

In my experience, three activities, a song, and a snack nicely fill the 1 hour and 15 minutes I plan for my Take-Your-Parent-to-School celebration.

I'd love to show you my work.
May I show you...

-
-
-

I'd love to show you my work.
May I show you...

-
-
-

I'd love to show you my work.
May I show you...

-
-
-

I'd love to show you my work.
May I show you...

-
-
-

Template for making work cards so children can list activities
they will show their parents at a Take-Your-Parent-to-School day

Spring Fling Class Picnic

Each spring, the families of the children in my class are invited to our classroom picnic, the Spring Fling. This is a partner event to our Winter Celebration, and allows the chance for a different guest to attend. As with the Winter Celebration, I plan ahead; I disclose the time and date of the Spring Fling in my weekly newsletter about eight weeks in advance, and follow up with weekly reminders. Parents and other guests appreciate the ample notice; they can request time off from employers well in advance, increasing the likelihood they'll be able to attend the event. For the same reason, I limit the event to two hours.

I plan many activities for the event so the adults have a chance to interact with the children as well as with each other. Typically there is a craft project (usually recycled paper pulp sculpted in cookie cutters) and a cooking project (often Ice Cream in a Bag, page 41). We plan for an outdoor event, but should the weather be uncooperative, we have a backup plan—an indoor "board game picnic" where children and guests engage in a variety of "tournaments."

I send out an invitation and ask for an RSVP; this helps me ensure that each child has a guest with whom to share the event. In the case that a child's family member is unable to attend, we can call on an older sibling within the school or a staff member to be the child's special guest.

Spring Fling invitation:

Please join us for our Spring Fling!

On Friday, May 13, we will host our Spring Fling. Please join us for our class picnic from 10:00 – 12:00. Due to limited space in our classroom, should we need to picnic inside, each child may invite only one adult to attend.

Each child will need to bring a disposable bag lunch for him/herself and a guest. Bubbles, kites, sidewalk chalk, and outdoor toys are welcome.

The schedule is as follows:
10:00 playground, free play, and papermaking craft
10:30 prepare for lunch
11:00 picnic lunch with a guest
11:30 making ice cream with our guests
12:00 return to our regular schedule

We hope to see you there!

_ _ _ _ _ _ _ _ _ _ _ _ _ _ _ _ _ _ _

Please RSVP

I, _____(Guest's name)_____,will be
_____(Child's name)_____ 's guest at the Spring Fling on May 13 at 10:00.

School-Wide Events

School-wide events range from musical performances to pancake feeds, carnivals to curriculum nights ("math night" or "reading night"). Truly, the event possibilities are only limited by space, resources, and the leadership of someone with the tenacity and creative energies to envision the event and bring it to fruition. I personally have a passion for the arts, so I have developed three school-wide events to which I am dearly attached: Paints and Parfaits, Poetry Slam, and our all-school play.

Paints and Parfaits — a Visual Art Exhibition

Paints and Parfaits is a visual art exhibition that occurs one morning each December from 7:30–8:30 am. Every student in the school (all 660 of them!), ranging in age from 3 to 11, has at least one piece of artwork on display in the gym or in the hallways of the school. The art pieces are all matted and labeled with the students' names. Children and their families roam the hallways admiring the artwork while eating yogurt parfaits. Vince Guaraldi jazz music plays over the PA system, and teachers dressed in black and white serve as "docents."

Parents, teachers, and children alike enjoy the colorful, relaxed feel of a day that begins in visual beauty, smooth jazz, and lighthearted conversation. For that one hour once a year, my school building becomes a gallery for art and connections.

Poetry Readings

The Poetry Slam is an annual evening event during which children and their families participate in non-competitive poetry readings. I turn one of the school's classrooms into a café-style environment with LED tea light candles, a music riser stage, and a donated microphone and speaker system. Children register in advance for a time slot in which to perform at the slam. Typically, 100–150 children and parents attend this event.

Every child in my school, from preschool through fifth grade, is invited to attend and read original poetry or poetic works created by others. They can read alone, or with a friend, parent, or family member. Parents participate by helping children choose pieces to read aloud, listening as they practice, attending as audience members, or often co-presenting on stage with the younger children. Occasionally, a teacher will create a piece of original poetry and dazzle the audience of children, parents, and colleagues. It's always delightful for the children to see a teacher in the role of poet, and an equal joy when children share funny poetry about their school and teachers! This experience occurs in conjunction with our school's pancake feed for an evening of Pancakes and Poetry … and apparently alliteration!

Poetry Slam Invitation published in the school newsletter:

You're Invited to Montclair's Ninth Annual Poetry Slam!

Please join us between 5 p.m. and 7 p.m. on January 26 for an evening of poetry. Students are invited to perform original or published works of poetry in a warm "coffee house" setting. Our "Slam" is a non-competitive event and all Montclair Students are welcome to participate.

Punctuate your evening of Montclair fun by joining the PTO at the Pancake Dinner held in the gym! That's twice the fun with Poetry and Pancakes!

After submitting the registration, students will be assigned a 15-minute session in which to perform. You will receive a confirmation to let you know when and where your child's performance will occur.

Students and adults are asked to arrive at least 5 minutes prior to their scheduled session and are requested to wait until the previous performance is complete before entering.

Poetry Slam Invitation, continued

Students:
I will participate by:
_____Performing my original work
_____Performing another person's work
_____Performing with a partner (another student or adult)
        Partner's Name _____
_____Being part of the audience

Adults:
_____I can help set up the room(s) at 4:30 p.m.
_____I can help take down the room(s) at 7:00 p.m.

Please return this registration by January 20 to the envelope in the office marked "Poetry Slam."

Name_____
Grade _____Teacher_____
Number performing/attending_____
Parent Signature_____

Children's Play — Montclair Community Theater

My greatest effort in community building comes in writing and directing an annual play for children in kindergarten through 5th grade—Montclair Community Theater. Each year I adapt a different children's book for the stage. Approximately 100–150 children participate in the cast and crew. Parents and families help children create costumes, build props and scenery, sell student-designed T-shirts, sell the children's book upon which the play is based, and host a cast and crew party to celebrate the successful production of our play.

The event has two performances to enable the entire student body and staff, as well as families, to attend. To see this large group of children of various ages and their families, all working together to create a cooperative stage production, is to witness an astonishing demonstration of community.

Likewise, it creates a safe environment for learners of all types to find their voice. Nick's mom was astounded by Nick's poise and ease on the stage.

Even my district superintendent complemented him on his performance after they left the stage together. (Yes! I invited my superintendent to perform in a cameo performance, and he accepted. Behold the reach of Elementary School Community Theater!)

Parent volunteers watch a Montclair Community Theater dress rehearsal

Beyond School Walls — Engagement in the Greater Community

Though school property is an obvious setting for social opportunities, I encourage you to think beyond school walls. Opening your personal life or your home to families adds another dimension to the relationship. Though this may seem like an intrusion into your private life, the reality is that your address, phone number, and other details aren't as private as you may think—a simple internet search will reveal a great many things.

Children have a natural curiosity about the lives of their teachers; many often believe that school is their teacher's home and their life is one-dimensional—they are a teacher only. Glimpses of humanness reveal a great many other roles to children and their families—wife, husband, mother, father, grandmother, grandfather, motorcycle rider, kickboxer, musician, or whatever!

I believe those multiple roles provide opportunities for more connections—some purely social, like the mother who shared her "motorcycle momma" email when she found out I rode, and some as intimate as the parent who reached out for resources to explain cancer to a child when she learned I was a survivor. Bonds are formed when you find those common experiences; affection and greater engagement follow.

Front-Porch Trick-or-Treating

What? You invite families to your home? Isn't that an invasion of your privacy? Yes, I do invite children to come to my home for trick-or-treating, and no, no one has ever abused this by coming to my home uninvited at other times. Nor have they ever texted or called my cell phone number (published on the nametags that children wear on field trips). I believe the transparency I've offered through all my parent engagement activities fosters trust and respect, and helps ensure the lines of privacy aren't crossed.

My home has a lovely front porch. On Halloween night, I turn it into a pirate boat, invite my students and their families to come "set sail," and partake in "pirate's grog" (warm apple cider) and treats. Children excitedly (and sometimes shyly) tumble out of their parents' cars for some Halloween fun; they are astonished to learn that I don't live at school! They are even more surprised to see me, my husband, and my cats dressed in pirate costumes! Even families who don't celebrate Halloween still stop by for a little warm cider on a chilly autumn night. To my great delight, my former students often drive themselves to my front door on Halloween, eager to see if I might still be willing to serve up grog for high school students.

I publish the date of the event (Halloween night), the time we'll set sail, and my address and directions in my newsletter several weeks in advance, and then follow up with reminders. I provide several weeks of invitations to ensure all families have the opportunity to be included in the event.

Summer Bicycle Parade Fun

My own children often tease me about being "kid lonely" over the summer months when my students are enjoying summer break. So, on the Fourth of July, I open my front lawn to my students and their families. I host a neighborhood bicycle parade, and that morning, I watch as children from my classroom haul their bikes and scooters decorated with flags and streamers from minivans and SUVs. They join neighborhood children in an approximately one-mile ride through my neighborhood. Afterward, they return to my front lawn to refresh themselves with popsicles. Many families linger, chatting about summer adventures, while the children explore my yard and visit with my overly gregarious cat, Greyson.

As with other activities, I publish the date, time, and location of the bike parade in my weekly newsletter (in this case, at the end of the school year). On occasion, parents have also reminded each other of the event by posting it on private social media pages. I love to see my parent engagement efforts expanding in this way!

A family participates in the 4th of July bicycle parade

Chapter IX
Addressing Challenges Together:
A Team Approach

Justin is the apple of his parents' eyes. The love they have for him oozes through each interaction. His every word and action delights them; he is their world. To them, he is clearly perfect in every way. Then, he goes to school for the very first time, and learning isn't coming easily.

Tiffany is precocious, spunky, and guided by whim — one of those children who, in all honesty, drives you bananas! She's not kind to the other children, and developing friendships doesn't come naturally. When she is one-on-one with an adult, a much different picture develops. She's intelligent and wildly imaginative, but her peers prefer to avoid her. Her mother is hoping you have some solutions.

When Tanya's dad, Paul, was a child, school was an annoyance at best. He mistrusted teachers, who in turn did little to earn his respect. His most vivid school memory is being shamed by a teacher in front of the whole class. That child is now a father, and his daughter has been placed in your class.

The scenarios are endless.

The opportunities are as well.

I have some friends who regularly tease me about being a teacher. "What was it that attracted you to the profession? Was it: a) status, b) wealth, or c) ease of the work?"

My answer is, "None of the above. I just want to be a champion for the children in my classroom."

It seems in our culture that champions are often associated with wealth and status. Our champions are frequently sports figures, business moguls, and Hollywood stars. They are often larger-than-life personalities or individuals who overcome tremendous odds.

I believe teachers who arrive at classrooms every day are champions. We give talent, time, treasure, and care to children who we affectionately refer to as "our kids." We advocate for those children's interests. We celebrate when those children thrive and feel the pain when those children struggle.

Over the course of our careers, we build relationships with hundreds, if not thousands, of individuals: children, parents, colleagues, administrators, and community members. Some of these relationships develop naturally and flow with ease, while others present more of a trial.

As early childhood educators, we may be the first to tell parents that the child they perceived as perfect has learning differences. We may confront a parent whose greatest hope is that we'll have the "fix" for a child's social issues. Or we may be faced with developing a relationship with a parent who is disinclined to like or trust us.

Ultimately, the child's success is the desired outcome of education, and finding a way for children to be successful is our job. Maria Montessori wrote, "This is the new shining hope for humanity." (1988, p. 259)

Developing Trust

Search for any book, article, meme, or inspirational quote on relationships, and you will probably find the topic of trust. It is said to be the foundation of all relationships; if you trust someone, you believe them to have sincere intentions.

Imagine you are speaking to a group of new parents in a setting such as a curriculum night, open house, or new-parent meeting. With unabashed honesty you begin: "Hello, I am *(state your name)*. It is my goal to gain your confidence, entice, persuade, enlist, inspire, and intentionally connect with you so we, together, can work toward the best possible educational outcome for your child."

And then continue, "And, in return, I wish for you to trust me, speak honestly with me, direct your questions to me, and willingly partner with me through celebrations and challenges."

Feel free to employ these words or words of your own to express a straightforward approach toward developing a relationship with parents, and then act with the same earnestness. I suppose it is a heavy self-introduction, but I believe it is most effective to communicate with sincerity and act with consistency of belief. This doesn't mean you'll always agree with parents, and it certainly doesn't mean relationships will always be easy, but when you have created partnership and trust with parents, challenges will be surmounted more easily.

Transparency is an important aspect of trust. Don't keep your intentions around parent engagement a secret; be open with parents about your commitment to enhance the mutual relationship between you, them, and the child. Talk about the specific activities and experiences you plan to use to develop trust and build community. Tell parents that these relationships matter—not only do they form the "village" that raises the child, but as research shows, they can contribute to the child's success!

After you present your ideas, be open to parent questions, and pursue answers through honest dialogue. Avoid the tendency to make assumptions about other's intentions. We all too often assume the worst of situations by writing mental scripts about the motivations of others. Often direct communication will make our intentions clear and lead to greater social cohesion.

Trust is not built in a single moment. It needs to be developed; a relationship with someone is an ongoing endeavor. When building connections with parents, we can provide multiple opportunities for engagement and multiple points at which trust can be built. I call this strategy the Confetti Approach. You never know what piece will stick!

Speaking Frankly, but Delicately

Envision this scenario: Johnny is unhappy when he comes home from school. He says the work is hard and dumb. He says the kids are mean and dumb. He says he doesn't like school. As his teacher you often remark in newsletters and parent meetings that a strong rapport between parent and teacher helps children be successful. His parents have shown great interest and participated in the parent engagement activities and strategies you have suggested. They have embraced your partnership, and you have had numerous opportunities for positive encounters. Still, Johnny is struggling. You are concerned.

Johnny has difficulty mastering concepts despite multiple repetitions and strategies. He has challenges in his social interactions, including behavioral outbursts. A conversation with his parents seems inevitable and necessary. Perhaps they've been expecting this conversation.

Does a partnership mean that this will be an easy conversation? Not necessarily, but chances are it will be easier to approach challenging topics with a parent who is already a partner, rather than with a parent who is a stranger.

These conversations require an honest and direct delivery, tempered with large doses of delicacy and grace. The focus of the conversation is observable behaviors (for example, reading proficiency, math progress, or social skills), rather than guesses at motivations or feelings. Documentation, such as observation checklists, daily / weekly / monthly work records, quarterly progress reports, parent-teacher conference records, or archived emails are all helpful to have on hand. Hopefully these observations and your expectations have been shared prior to the conversation so that parents are not blindsided by your concerns.

I prefer to have these types of conversations in person, although my initial contact is usually established through an email. There are, however, occasions when time and circumstances do not allow for a face-to-face discussion, and the dialogue has to occur electronically. I choose not to call working parents during the day when neither party can devote their full attention to the conversation.

I begin my emails with a phrase like, "Hello, I just wanted to touch base about some observations in the classroom. Would you have time to meet, or is email easier for your schedule?"

This email communicates courtesy to the parent by providing options for methods of communication.

I begin with an observation of the child's successes. I like to call this a reflection of the "being" of the child. Perhaps the child showed kindness to a friend, or enjoyed dance activities. Observations of the things the child does well clearly communicate genuine concern for the child and demonstrate your ability to view the child positively.

Delivery of the concerns should reflect the "doings" of the child. Report observable, objective, and documented behaviors, and refrain from subjective accusations and absolutes such as "he always" and "she never."

When speaking in person, neutral, non-verbal communications and a calm demeanor express professionalism: besides concern, no feelings should enter the conversation. To ensure this, have the conversation at a time when you can stay calm—probably not at the end of a school day when a child's behavior has driven you to exasperation. A dismissal-time response to the question "How did she do today?" can rarely be delivered with an adequate amount of preparedness, effectiveness, or privacy.

One of the most difficult impulses to resist when discussing a child's challenging behavior is judging the parents. It is quite typical and often well-intended to attempt to understand where challenges began. However, there is seldom a single or uncomplicated root cause for challenging behavior. When we lack information, we tend to fill in the blanks and create explanations that, even when concluded in the most positive light, may be distorted or simply untrue.

Instead of making assumptions or speculations, it is better to ask direct questions. They may be something like:

- "What observations do you have of Lily's behavior when she's frustrated?"

- "How does Darren demonstrate persistence when learning something new?"
- "What is Jacob's attention like at soccer? Dance? At home when you give him directions?"
- "Is Tara interested in having you read to her at home?"
- "What helps Mario accept redirection from adults?"

There is more room for information to flow freely and honestly when a parent-teacher relationship has been built upon trust and transparency. In other words, a deliberate and well-established relationship with a child's parents makes it easier for both parent and teacher to approach one another with concerns. Both parties will feel a level of comfort in asking for clarification if more insight is required.

As teachers, it is our job to accept each child "warts and all" (as my grandmother would say). We should not dwell on information we have about a child's past. Even the well-intended teacher cannot control the myriad of conditions that influence a child's social, emotional, intellectual, or behavioral needs.

Instead, we must exercise empathy and use the wealth of information that experience, peers, experts, and parents provide us with to help a child be the most successful in our care. It may mean we have to let go of our own ego, needs, and expectations to pursue a path that better serves the development of the child.

Parallel Language and Expectations

When overcoming challenges and working with parents, parallel discussions at home and at school offer consistency for children. Common language developed by both parent and teacher reflects similar expectations: "Your mommy and I want you to have a good day at school with your friends by using kind words. Will you let us help you?"

The goal is specific, singular, and addresses one behavior at a time: in this case, kind words.

The question, "Will you let us help you?" is mirrored at home and school.

Both parent and teacher are transparent with the child and assure the child they are all working together, (the word "us" demonstrates this). The ongoing dialogue between parent, teacher, and child helps the child become aware of the commitment of parent and teacher working together, in support of one another and the child. And, yes, I specifically chose the word "ongoing."

You may develop deep relationships with the parents of a child with behavior or learning concerns, simply because of the amount of energy you are willing to put toward the child's success.

The role of "teacher" comes with a tremendous commitment. You will not know all the solutions, and you need not seek the answers alone.

Then What?

In an ideal scenario, the child described above would have a wealth of support from home and school, and the goal of "kind words" would also be met. Well, I can't tell you it will always happen, nor can I tell you that it will never happen. The reality is that humans have free will and children will, on occasion, exercise their discretion to act independently of their teachers' or parents' wishes. (Surprise!)

All learning challenges will not necessarily be remedied by a parent-teacher relationship. Behavior and learning are much more complex than can be addressed in a single conversation. Most likely, a dialogue will continue and be revisited. It may alter as you choose to focus upon a second issue if the first issue is resolved, and it may return even as the child moves on to new environments. Parents may reach out to you as children enter first or second grade when the family meets a new teacher. When those parents have reached out to me, I strongly encourage the development of the relationship with the new teacher.

One of my usual responses is, "There was once a time when I was a stranger to you and your child. I have confidence you'll develop a fine relationship with your child's new teacher." Intentional connections between children, parents, and teachers are powerful at all levels of a child's development.

Success for our children is the goal of a champion teacher. We contemplate strategies to help children as we drive home from school. We will talk and answer emails long after the school day ends. Sometimes the results are slow to manifest. Sometimes the results don't seem evident at all. But no effort is ever wasted. Champions have faith in the impact of their work.

Epilogue: I've Made a Difference

As educators, one of our greatest pleasures—and greatest responsibilities—is aiding families in raising their children.

"Wait! " you may exclaim. "I didn't plan on a career of that magnitude."

Too late! As a teacher you have the opportunity to be a significant influence on the life of a young child, and, by extension, that child's family. Put in Montessori terms, as you "follow the child," you will inevitably find the family. Montessori teachers, who frequently spend three years with a child, can't help but become a part of that family in ways both subtle and direct. A child's mind soaks up impressions from their environment, and the teacher's manner of speech, dress, and behavior are part of the environment that is absorbed by the child and reflected to their family.

This phenomenon goes both ways: as a teacher, you'll celebrate children's successes, worry about their distresses, and you will be touched by their lives, just as they will be touched by yours. If you cross paths with them as young adults, they may remember you, or perhaps they won't. Nonetheless, your impact will persist. Children may not remember the specific lessons, and they will probably never know the care you took to prepare those lessons to match the sensitive period of each unique child, but you will know that part of the foundation of their being was shaped during the time spent with you. Maria Montessori wrote:

> The teacher of children up to six years of age knows that she has helped mankind in an essential part of its formation. She may know nothing of the children's circumstances, except what they have told her freely in conversation; possibly she takes no interest in their future: whether they will go on to secondary schools and the university, or end their studies sooner; but she is happy in the

knowledge that in this formative period they were able to do what they had to do. She will be able to say: "I have served the spirits of those children, and they have fulfilled their development, and I kept them company in their experiences." (Montessori, 1967, p. 284)

There was a time when the village raised the child. Extended families and close-knit communities surrounded children as they grew. Now we live in highly mobile cultures where grandparents or other extended family may live thousands of miles away. Communities are ever-changing as neighbors come and go along with housing market trends. A teacher-parent partnership may be one thing that can remain the same for a child. As teachers, we have a responsibility to build that relationship—that village—with deliberate intention and attention, and to make the most of the time we have together. Providing countless opportunities for the development of relationships with parents and their children is a major part of the life of a teacher.

In building these connections, you will undoubtedly receive the satisfaction and joy of knowing that you made a difference. You were a positive and powerfully influential part of the child's village. You were the "confetti thrower" in the parade of young lives that crossed your threshold!

Have fun!

Learn lots!

Make new friends!

References

Anik, L., Aknin, L. B., Norton, M. I. & Dunn, E. W. (2009). Feeling Good about Giving: The Benefits (and Costs) of Self-Interested Charitable Behavior (Working paper No. 10 – 012). Harvard Business School.

Asch, F. (1978). Bear Books. NY: Simon and Schuster.

Breuning, L. G. (2012). Meet Your Happy Chemicals. Retrieved from https://www.psychologytoday.com/files/attachments/59029/happy-chemicals.pdf

Center for Public Education (2011, August 30). Back to School: How Parent Involvement Affects Student Achievement. Retrieved from http://www.centerforpubliceducation.org/research/back-school-how-parent-involvement-affects-student-achievement

Clark, B., (Producer and Director). (1983). *A Christmas Story*. [Motion picture]. USA: Metro-Goldwyn-Mayer.

Cotton, K. & Wikelund, K. (1989), Parent Involvement in Education. Regional Educational Laboratory Northwest, School Improvement Research.

Duke, N.K. (2003). Information Books in Early Childhood. National Association for the Education of Young Children. Retrieved from http://docplayer.net/20751205-Information-books-in-early-childhood.html

Freeman, D. (1968). *Corduroy*. NY: Viking Press.

Gottman, J.M. (2001). *The Relationship Cure*. NY: Harmony.

Harvard Family Research Project (2010). *Parent-Teacher Conference Tip Sheets for Principals, Teachers and Parents*. MA: Harvard Graduate School of Education.

Henderson, A. T. & Mapp, K. L. (2002). *A New Wave of Evidence: The Impact of School, Family, and Community Connections On Student Achievement*. TX: Southwest Educational Development Laboratory.

Kraftwohl, D.R., Bloom, B.S. & Masia, B.B. (1973). *Taxonomy of Educational Objectives, the Classification of Educational Goals. Handbook II: Affective Domain*. NY: David McKay Co., Inc.

Macleod, D. (2012, February 19). Engagement vs. Involvement. Retrieved from https://www.thoughtexchange.com/engagement-vs-involvement/

Michigan Department of Education. (2002, March). What Research Says about Parent Involvement in Children's Education in Relation to Academic Achievement. http://www.chsd.us/barryton/docs/Parent_Involvement_ Guide.pdf

Montessori, M. (1967). *The Absorbent Mind*. NY: Henry Holt and Company.

Montessori, M. (1988). *The Absorbent Mind*. Oxford, England: Clio Press.

Montessori, M. (1948). *The Discovery of the Child*. Madras, India: Kalakshetra Press.

Montessori, M. (1990). *The Discovery of the Child*. Oxford, England: Clio Press.

Montessori, M. (1948). *To Educate the Human Potential*. Madras, India: Kalakshetra Press.

Montessori, M. (1946). *Education for a New World*. Madras, India: Kalakshetra Press.

Montessori, M. (1971). *The Four Planes of Education*. Amsterdam, Netherlands: Association Montessori Internationale.

Montessori, M. (1965). *Spontaneous Activity in Education*. NY: Schocken.

Muth, J. (2003). *Stone Soup*. NY: Scholastic Press.

National PTA. (2000). *Building Successful Partnerships: A Guide for Developing Parent and Family Involvement Programs*. IN: National Education Service.

Sagan, C., Druyan, A., & Tyson, N. D. (2013). *Cosmos*. NY: Ballantine Books Trade Paperbacks.

Sendak, M. (1962). *Chicken Soup with Rice: A book of months*. NY: HarperCollins Publishers.

Sensenbaugh, R., & Reading, E. (1996). Phonemic Awareness an Important Early Step in Learning to Read. IN: ERIC Clearinghouse on Reading, English, and Communication.

Van Petten, V. (2011, November 2). 5 Ways to Make a Killer First Impression. Retrieved from http://www.forbes.com/sites/yec/2011/11/02/5-ways-to-make-a-killer-first-impression/#5a22eb8f10ce

Weiss, H., Caspe, M. & Lopez, M. E. (2006, Spring). Family Involvement in Early Childhood Education. Family Involvement Makes a Difference. Retrieved from www.hfrp.org/publications-resources/browse-ourpublications/family-involvement-in-early-childhood-education

Weller, C. (2013, July 12). Nostalgia Is Good For You: When We Reminisce, Life Feels More Meaningful and Death Less Frightening. Retrieved from https://www.medicaldaily.com/nostalgia-good-you-when-we-reminisce-life-feels-more-meaningful-and-death-less-frightening-247627

Williams, M. (2014), *The Velveteen Rabbit*. NY: Penguin Random House.

Wordsworth, W. (n.d.). I Wandered Lonely as a Cloud. Retrieved from https://www.poetryfoundation.org/poems/45521/i-wandered-lonely-as-a-cloud

130

Testimonials

You will not find a teacher with better parent engagement skills and activities than Mrs. Harman. Whether through Bud the Bear, classroom newsletters, or simply parent-teacher conferences, time and again she has demonstrated her passion for learning and young people's development through her partnership with parents. We have been blessed to have both of our daughters under Mrs. Harman's wing and they are better, more enlightened girls as a result.

Mark Kratina — Author of The Playground

When I first met Dorothy Harman, I was enchanted by her beautiful spirit and energy. As we have become friends, I have found that her bright smile and humor are fed by her passion for her family, for supporting young children as they grow and learn, and for contributing to a world where a sense of oneness among all people is possible. *Intentional Connections* is her contribution to that world as she provides a wealth of ideas for helping teachers intentionally build connections with families of the children they serve.

Joyce Kinney, MA Ed, Early Childhood Specialist

Dorothy Harman has taken her years of teaching experience and building community among children and parents and turned it into a beautiful hands-on guide for teachers. Her ideas are creative, inspiring, and can be put into action right away. Maria Montessori said that early education is the key to the betterment of society. Dorothy's love of working with children and parents is evident. Dorothy has created a dynamic masterpiece that should be in every teacher's hands. It all begins with building a family within a family.

Tiffany Fennig, Montessori Resource Teacher
Bunche Montessori Early Childhood Center, Fort Wayne, Indiana

---

During our first visit to Mrs. Harman's classroom, our daughters felt so welcomed and comfortable, they wanted to start attending that very day! We love the environment Mrs. Harman has created and are so pleased with the balance of Montessori practices accompanied by activities like music, movement, cooking, Sign Language, Spanish, and Practical Life skills. Our daughters actually argue over who is doing the dinner dishes in the evening! It's great to see our children enjoy learning in so many different ways. Thank you, Mrs. Harman.

Suzanne Schumaker, Substitute Teacher

I liked taking Bud to places like church, the chiropractor, and dance lessons because we got to get him dressed and take his picture.

Delia (age 5), Mrs. Harman's current student

It was fun helping my sister take care of Bud and picking out his outfits.

Sadie (age 4), Montessori student and sister in the neighboring classroom

---

We could not have asked for a more understanding and loving teacher than Mrs. Harman for our children's early childhood education. She understood our daughter's need to be challenged academically and fostered her interest in performing arts. Our daughter has performed in three national tours and gives Mrs. Harman credit for her start in theatre. Our son had a stronger interest in hockey than school. Mrs. Harman adapted his lessons around the sport. Circles became hockey pucks and math lessons were incorporated from game scores. She understood our kids and could engage both of them with her lessons. It takes a village to raise kids and we are grateful to have Mrs. Harman in our village. My hope for teachers reading this book is that they are able gain skills to give families that same love and understanding.

Jen Johnson, parent

I have known Dorothy for 17 years. I have seen the passion she has for her students and their families lived out on a daily basis. Her desire to have children and their parents interact on many different levels is her calling and I am beyond excited to see her passion be expressed in written form.

Tammy Schill, Certified Nursing Assistant
Neihardt Elementary School

Ms. Harman sets the standard when it comes to building meaningful parent-teacher relationships. My family was fortunate to have both our children in her class for a total of 7 years. She made a lasting impact on our lives. Without question her ability to build strong relationships is one of the cornerstones to her success and makes her one of the leading educators in Montessori. She is equally comfortable in the classroom with children and in the community interacting with adults; in both situations her leadership creates an enjoyable environment. Anyone who is fortunate enough to read this book will benefit from her techniques and wisdom.

Jana Saddler and the Waughn Family

We have been blessed to know Mrs. Harman for almost nine years. Both our children were in her early childhood classroom at Montclair Elementary. Mrs. Harman is a kind soul who effortlessly implements the philosophy of Maria Montessori. Our children thrived under Mrs. Harman's direction … she provided a loving and productive classroom environment and included families in the process to provide a cohesive approach. We consider ourselves extremely lucky to have been placed with Mrs. Harman so many years ago.

Lynette Rohlfs, parent

Mrs. Harman has always been a great role model to both me and all the kids she has taught. She taught me how to count, stay on task, and most importantly to be kind to one another. We still have a great connection such as going to her house on the 4th of July and on Halloween for trick-or-treating. The skills she has taught me in the past will help me in the present and future.

Reagan Rohlfs (age 12), former student

Mrs. Harman is really nice and cares about other people. She is a good teacher and always knows what stuff is. Her house is really fun when we go for Halloween and drinking apple cider. Also, riding bikes in her parade for the 4th of July is fun. She makes learning fun and taught me the alphabet. She plays in a musical band that is really good and we watched them play Vala Pumpkin Patch.

Mason Rohlfs (age 10), former student

Acknowledgments

I have an abundance of gratitude for all the people who have supported and encouraged me in the writing of this book.

My deepest thanks to my husband, Chris, whose patience and pizza made this work possible and to Carol Sapp and Brenda Peters, who made it beautiful.

I would like to express my most sincere appreciation to the following, who have all taught me the meaning of connections.

My children, family, friends and colleagues.

Tobey, who told me I had a vision to share.

My friends at Parent Child Press — Joe, Jane C., Carey,
Irene, Shannon, Jane J., and Ann.

The Montessori community, Millard Public Schools, and Unity teachings.

And the many children and
their families who have transformed my work.

About the Author

Dorothy Harman is an early childhood teacher in a public Montessori school (Montclair Elementary School) in Omaha, Nebraska. She is also an early childhood teacher-trainer at Mid-America Montessori Teachers' Training Institute in Omaha, and a consultant/instructor at the University of Nebraska, Kearney. She holds a Masters in Education degree from Doane College and a second Masters in Education with an Emphasis in Creative Arts from Lesley University. She is a lifetime member of the American Montessori Society and a member of the International Montessori Council.

She lives with her husband (Chris), and enjoys visits with her two children (Alicia and Anthony), two stepdaughters (Katina and Lara), two granddaughters (Adelya and Nevia) and her three cats (Greyson, Timmy and 24-pound orange tabby Pumpkin).

When she is not teaching, training teachers, or presenting at national education conferences, Dorothy enjoys writing, speaking to her church congregation, performing with several bands, and riding her purple motorcycle.